Praise for DARRYL CUNNINGHAM

'Deals with some of the most urgent debates in science using pictures, speech bubbles and comic-strip layouts... sorting facts from fiction and presenting complex information in a highly accessible way.'
Observer

'Cunningham's charming artwork complements his concise arguments... his stark lines and simple layouts give his comic the feel of a scientific analysis. The artwork is uncluttered, leaving little to distract the reader from the exposition, delivered in stripped-back, staccato prose.'
New Scientist

'He has managed to distil the arguments into a wonderfully clear and concise form... a great primer for those seeking arguments to undermine their *Daily Express*-reading uncle.'
Herald Scotland

'It's clear and straightforward at all times, making complex issues simple, but never simplistic.'
Headline Environment

'His style is cartoony and raw, but manages to be full of expression and also very evocative. Even if you haven't tried to read something in comic format before, you'll find this easy to follow on the one hand, and thought-provoking on the other.'
Bradford Telegraph & Argus

'Cunningham's art has clean lines and a continuity that is often graceful, charming and endearing. He speaks with quiet authority on his subjects, but is careful to cite a whole range of sources and research papers.'
Independent

'Brilliantly presented, and customarily classy... Cunningham delivering his message with style, great art, even moments of outright comedy.'
Forbidden Planet

'It's a meticulous picking apart of the ridiculous web of half-baked facts and fiction that's often woven around one or two grains of truth, usually completely taken and distorted totally out

Also by Darryl Cunningham

'A lovely book which combines its no-nonsense approach with a funny, pro-science attitude.'
Edzard Ernst, *The Pulse*

'Cunningham projects a quietly authoritative voice throughout. Artistically, his clean lines and his deceptively simple cartooning style perfectly complement the clarity inherent in the delivery of his carefully considered points. *Science Tales* manages to be somehow simultaneously both succinct and substantive, and a fierce and intelligent promoter of the scientific process over blind superstition and baseless supposition.'
Broken Frontier

'A fantastic nonfiction comic book about science, scepticism and denial. Cunningham has a real gift for making complex subjects simple. If you're trying to discuss these subjects with smart but misguided friends and loved ones, this book might hold the key to real dialogue.'
Cory Doctorow, *Boing Boing*

'Cunningham is admirably erudite… The result is persuasive rhetoric: popular science not overly technical, but communicated clearly and with conviction. Cunningham writes with the courtroom eloquence of the prosecuting barrister, denouncing the accused in capital letters, his words as precise as his drawing style is hard-edged.'
Graphic Medicine

'An eye-catching way to get across the important message that a science-based approach to understanding makes far more sense than one that is evidence-free. Cunningham draws out the fictions and lays bare the facts.'
Chemistry World

DARRYL CUNNINGHAM
SUPERCRASH
HOW TO HIJACK THE GLOBAL ECONOMY

First published in 2014 by

Myriad Editions
59 Lansdowne Place
Brighton BN3 1FL, UK

www.myriadeditions.com

This edition published in 2014

1 3 5 7 9 10 8 6 4 2

A CIP catalogue record for this book is available from
the British Library.

ISBN: 978-1-908434-43-2

Printed in Latvia on paper sourced from sustainable forests.

CONTENTS :

ACKNOWLEDGEMENTS:

I had a lot of help writing *Supercrash*. I owe a huge debt of gratitude to the many writers whose work I read when in the long process of research. Without them this book would be very light on information. So thanks to Anne C. Heller, Jennifer Burns, Charles Ferguson, John Lancaster, Gillian Tett, Bethany McLean, Joe Nocera, Michael Lewis, Chris Mooney, Joseph Stiglitz, Gary Weiss, and, of course, Ayn Rand herself. It's well worth reading all of the books I've used as source material for *Supercrash*.

Others who gave me help and support in various ways were Paul Gravett, Nick Abadzis, Ian Williams, Simon Fraser, Lizz Lunney, Sarah McIntyre, Graham Johnstone, Tom Spurgeon, Eric Orchard, Julie Crack, Jon Ronson, Nye Wright, Vivekanand Sridhar, Jonathan Edwards, and my parents.

Also thanks to Candida Lacey, Adrian Weston, Linda McQueen, and everyone at Myriad Editions. A particularly big thanks to my editor Corinne Pearlman for her endless patience and hard work.

FOREWORD

This book is inspired by a writer and novelist, largely unknown in Europe. Even in the United States, where she is most famous, she is surely a fringe thinker. Why, with all that there is to say about politics and finance in the modern world, did I start with Ayn Rand?

I first read about Ayn Rand when I was in my twenties. Her upside-down moral philosophy of Objectivism – selfishness is a virtue and altruism a moral failing – was so opposed to everything I believed that I was drawn to her with a mixture of horror and fascination. It was, and still is, shocking to me that anyone could be so nakedly self-serving.

Rand hits a nerve with people. We either reject her beliefs totally or embrace them wholeheartedly. There is no middle ground. We can't be indifferent to her philosophy. If we are to the left, we'll take her writings as a personal attack. If we are on the far right, she will outline many of our deepest inner beliefs more clearly than we have ever thought about them ourselves.

Rand sells. At least, in America she sells. Two of her novels, *The Fountainhead* (1943), and *Atlas Shrugged* (1957), typically sell more than 300,000 copies a year. Since the 2008 financial crisis, sales of her apocalyptic novel, *Atlas Shrugged*, have tripled. A total of 600,000 copies of the book were sold in 2009. In the United States more than 13 million copies of these two books are in circulation.

I wrote about Ayn Rand for the same reasons that she is so popular with those on the political right: because she is emblematic of so much deeply right-wing thinking. Her life and writing demonstrate a conservatism boiled down to its purest essence, both good and bad: individualism, self-reliance, and selfishness.

Rand was my gateway into understanding not just the the conservative mind, but how this mindset has brought about the triumph of neo-liberal politics over the last thirty years – the encouragement of free trade and open markets, privatisation, deregulation, and the extension of the role of the private sector in modern society. These elements all culminated in the catastrophic financial crisis of 2008 and human costs on a massive scale, affecting everyone from the middle classes to the very poorest across the globe.

This book is split into three sections. The first section is a biography of Ayn Rand. As well as chronicling the main events of the author's life, it outlines her novels and her philosophy of Objectivism, and demonstrates the huge influence she had, not just on the American political right as a whole, but specifically on one individual who was a key player in the events leading to the crisis.

The second section details the economic crisis itself. It explains how the trade in derivatives (a kind of insurance that can also be used for speculation and gambling), combined with the collapse of the US housing market, sheer greed amongst those in the banking sector and mortgage industry, and weak government regulation, brought the world's economy to its knees.

The third section is an overview of where we are today, starting with a look at the psychology of conservative and liberal thinking. What are the strengths and weaknesses of these two very different political persuasions? What does science tell us about them?

This last section also considers the vanishing influence of the left, the scapegoating of the poor and minorities as a response to the crisis, and how this scapegoating has contributed to the rise of both the Tea Party movement in the United States, and UKIP in the United Kingdom.

Ayn Rand understood that politics and economics have a moral dimension. It's never the case that business is just business. It's always personal. But the different approaches to morality held by the left and the right inevitably lead to opposing outcomes. For the last thirty years the political right have been in ascendance in the West, and they have shaped the world with their own vision of morality. In a democratic state where we have the power of the vote, surely it is time we take back control from those who see virtue in the acquisition of money over equality for all?

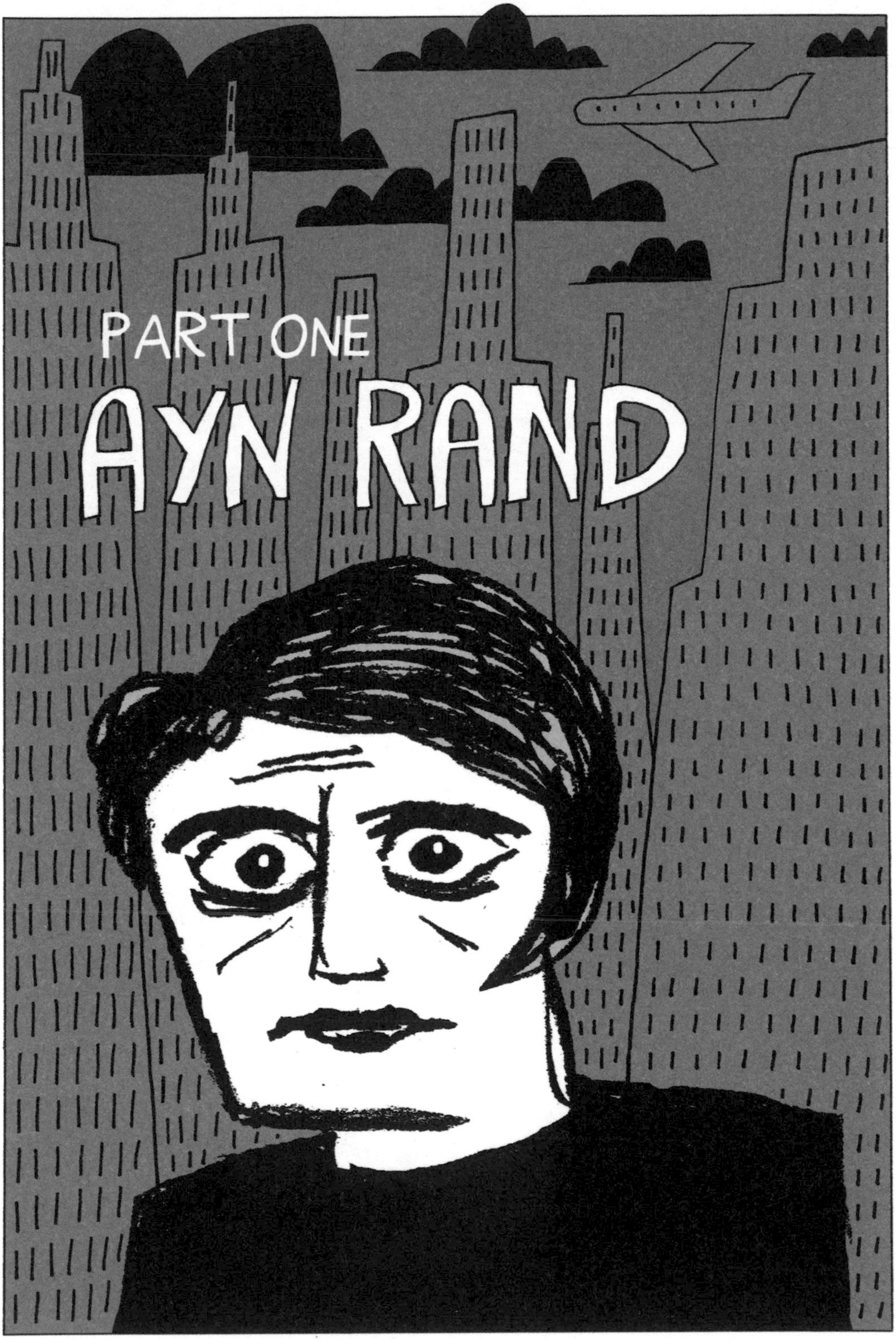
PART ONE
AYN RAND

AYN RAND WAS BORN ALISA ROSENBAUM IN ST PETERSBURG, RUSSIA, ON FEBRUARY 2, 1905.

HER FATHER, ZINOVY, WAS A CHEMIST WHO OWNED THE SHOP BELOW THE FAMILY'S APARTMENT.

HER MOTHER, ANNA, WAS A SOCIAL CLIMBER WHO, IT APPEARED, CARED LITTLE FOR HER DAUGHTERS.

ONE DAY, WHEN RAND WAS ABOUT FIVE, HER MOTHER CAME INTO THE PLAYROOM WHERE SHE AND HER SISTER HAD STREWN THEIR TOYS.

LOOK AT THIS MESS! YOU WILL HAVE TO CHOOSE SOME OF THESE TOYS TO PUT AWAY AND SOME TO KEEP AND PLAY WITH NOW.

IN A YEAR, YOU CAN TRADE THE TOYS YOU KEPT FOR THOSE YOU HAVE PUT AWAY.

RAND IMAGINED THE PLEASURE SHE WOULD GET WHEN HER FAVOURITE TOYS WERE EVENTUALLY RETURNED.

SO SHE HANDED OVER HER BEST-LOVED PLAYTHINGS...

INCLUDING A PAINTED MECHANICAL WIND-UP CHICKEN.

ONE YEAR LATER.

MOMMA! ISN'T IT TIME NOW FOR MY TOYS TO BE RETURNED TO ME?

POOR CHILD. I GAVE YOUR TOYS TO THE ORPHANAGE. IF YOU REALLY HAD WANTED THEM, YOU WOULDN'T HAVE HANDED THEM OVER IN THE FIRST PLACE.

WHAT?

RAND WAS A BRIGHT, SURLY CHILD, NOTABLE FOR HER DARK, PIERCING EYES AND DAMNING OPINIONS.

WHEN SHE WAS ASKED AT SCHOOL TO WRITE AN ESSAY ON WHY BEING A CHILD WAS A JOYOUS EXPERIENCE...

SHE INSTEAD WROTE A SCATHING DENUNCIATION OF CHILDHOOD.

I WOULD PREFER AN INTELLIGENT HELL TO A STUPID PARADISE.*

* RAND QUOTED PASCAL IN HER ESSAY.

RAND WOULD HAVE LIKED TO HAVE FRIENDS, BUT HER TENDENCY TO DISMISS ALL THOSE WHO DIDN'T MIRROR HER THOUGHTS EXACTLY PRECLUDED THIS...

A PATTERN SHE WOULD REPEAT ALL HER LIFE.

IN 1917, THE ROSENBAUMS' COMFORTABLE BOURGEOIS EXISTENCE, WITH THEIR COOK, MAID, NURSE AND GOVERNESS, WAS SWEPT AWAY IN THE TURMOIL OF THE RUSSIAN REVOLUTION.

ZINOVY'S PHARMACY WAS SEIZED BY THE BOLSHEVIKS.

I CLAIM THIS PLACE IN THE NAME OF THE PEOPLE.

HOPING TO SET UP ANOTHER BUSINESS, ZINOVY TOOK HIS FAMILY TO THE CRIMEA. IT WAS HIS BELIEF THAT IT WAS ONLY A MATTER OF TIME BEFORE THE BOLSHEVIK REGIME COLLAPSED.

THEY MOVED INTO A SMALL, UNHEATED HOUSE IN YEVPATORIA, ON THE BLACK SEA COAST.

IT'S FREEZING.

THE WAR RAGED ALL AROUND THEM. THE TOWN CHANGED HANDS FOUR OR FIVE TIMES IN THE THREE YEARS THE ROSENBAUMS WERE THERE.

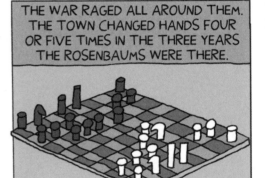

FINALLY THE RED ARMY ACHIEVED COMPLETE VICTORY OVER THE WHITE RUSSIANS.

IN 1921, HAVING EXHAUSTED ALL POSSIBILITIES OF EMPLOYMENT, THE ROSENBAUMS MADE THE LONG JOURNEY BACK TO ST PETERSBURG.

ST PETERSBURG WAS A CITY MUCH CHANGED. THE POPULATION HAD SHRUNK BY TWO-THIRDS.

THE ROSENBAUMS HAD TO MOVE INTO A SINGLE ROOM IN THEIR OLD APARTMENT, NOW OCCUPIED BY A SIGN-PAINTER AND HIS WIFE.

THERE WAS NO ELECTRICITY OR HOT WATER. FOOD WAS STRICTLY RATIONED. CROWDS OF UNEMPLOYED WORKERS AND DEMOBBED RED ARMY SOLDIERS ROAMED THE STREETS.

RAND ALWAYS CLAIMED THAT THE DETAILS OF HER LIFE HAD NOTHING TO DO WITH THE TENETS OF HER PHILOSOPHY.

DON'T ASK ME ABOUT MY CHILDHOOD, MY FRIENDS, MY FAMILY, OR MY FEELINGS. ASK ME ABOUT THE THINGS I THINK.

BUT IT IS CLEAR THAT HER VIEWS OF THE BRUTE MASSES AS A TERRIFYING, ROBBING HORDE WERE FORMED DURING THIS TIME.

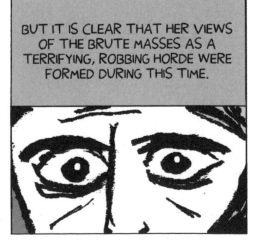

RAND LEFT FOR AMERICA IN 1926, JUST BEFORE HER TWENTY-FIRST BIRTHDAY.

SHE HAD A STAMPED PASSPORT AND THE SPONSORSHIP OF RELATIVES OF HER MOTHER IN CHICAGO.

THROUGHOUT HER CHILDHOOD, RAND HAD DREAMED OF ESCAPING TO AMERICA. SHE BELIEVED THIS WAS THE ONLY COUNTRY WHERE HER DETERMINED INDIVIDUALISM COULD FLOURISH.

WHEN RAND FIRST SAW THE SKYSCRAPERS OF NEW YORK, SHE WAS MOVED TO A RARE DISPLAY OF EMOTION.

MY TEARS THAT DAY WERE THE TEARS OF SPLENDOUR.

LATER IN LIFE, RAND PORTRAYED HERSELF AS A SELF-CREATED WOMAN WHOSE SUCCESS CAME ABOUT ENTIRELY THROUGH HER OWN INDOMITABLE WILL.

NO ONE HELPED ME, NOR DID I THINK IT WAS ANYONE'S DUTY TO HELP ME.

YET SHE WAS HELPED BY MANY PEOPLE DURING THOSE EARLY YEARS.

SHE STAYED WITH HER RELATIVES IN CHICAGO FOR SIX MONTHS.

SHE FAILED TO REPAY, OR EVEN OFFER TO REPAY, SMALL LOANS GIVEN TO HER.

GOOD LUCK.

THE FAMILY, THROUGH THEIR CONNECTIONS WITH A FILM DISTRIBUTOR, MANAGED TO SUPPLY RAND WITH A LETTER OF INTRODUCTION TO THE DEMILLE ORGANISATION IN HOLLYWOOD.

THEY ALSO PAID FOR HER TRAIN FARE TO CALIFORNIA AND INITIAL LIVING EXPENSES.

NONE OF THIS HELP WAS ACKNOWLEDGED BY RAND IN HER LATER YEARS.

ALMOST IMMEDIATELY ON ARRIVING IN HOLLYWOOD, RAND'S FIERCE WILL TO SUCCEED BROUGHT HER GOOD FORTUNE.

EITHER BY ACCIDENT OR DESIGN, SHE MANAGED TO CROSS PATHS WITH THE PRODUCER AND DIRECTOR CECIL B. DEMILLE.

? MR DEMILLE!

DEMILLE WAS SO IMPRESSED BY RAND THAT HE GAVE HER A JOB AS AN EXTRA IN 'THE KING OF KINGS'.

SHE REFUSED TO TAKE THE ROLE OF A BEGGAR WOMAN, PLAYING INSTEAD A MEMBER OF THE ROMAN NOBILITY.

RAND TOLD DEMILLE THAT SHE WANTED TO BE A WRITER AND THAT SHE HAD BROUGHT A STACK OF MOVIE SCENARIOS WITH HER FROM CHICAGO.

THE PRODUCER SENT HER TO THE HEAD OF HIS STORY DEPARTMENT.

THESE STORIES ARE FAR-FETCHED AND THE CHARACTERS ARE NOT HUMAN ENOUGH.

MORE THAN THIRTY YEARS LATER, RAND TOLD A FRIEND...

I STILL HATE THAT WOMAN TO THIS DAY.

DEMILLE HIRED RAND AS A JUNIOR SCREENWRITER ANYWAY.

RAND FIRST SAW FRANK O'CONNOR ON THE SET OF 'THE KING OF KINGS'.

O'CONNOR WAS ALSO WORKING AS AN EXTRA.

THAT MAN. SO HANDSOME.

WITH HER USUAL SINGLE-MINDED RESOLVE, SHE SET OUT TO CATCH O'CONNOR.

THE COUPLE WERE MARRIED IN
LOS ANGELES ON APRIL 15, 1929.

O'CONNOR WAS A GENIAL,
GOOD-LOOKING MAN, PATIENT
AND HUMOROUS.

AS HE TOOK LITTLE PART IN
HER INTELLECTUAL INTERESTS,
OBSERVERS MAY HAVE THOUGHT
FRANK A MERELY ORNAMENTAL
PART OF RAND'S LIFE.

BUT, FOR RAND, FRANK'S ROLE
WAS INVALUABLE. HE WAS BOTH
HER SUPPORT AND HER SHIELD
AGAINST THE OUTSIDE WORLD.

RAND'S FIRST SUCCESS AS A WRITER
CAME WITH THE SALE OF HER
SCREENPLAY 'RED PAWN', ALTHOUGH
IT WAS NEVER PRODUCED.

THEN CAME THE COURTROOM
DRAMA 'NIGHT OF JANUARY
16TH', FIRST STAGED IN
HOLLYWOOD, AND THEN
LATER ON BROADWAY.

THE PLAY HAD AN INTERESTING GIMMICK. EACH NIGHT, A JURY WAS SELECTED FROM THE AUDIENCE...

AND ONE OF TWO DIFFERENT ENDINGS WOULD THEN BE PERFORMED, DEPENDING ON THE JURY'S VERDICT.

NOT GUILTY.

RAND AND O'CONNOR MOVED TO NEW YORK FOR THE BROADWAY PRODUCTION. IN THE YEARS SINCE SHE HAD LAST BEEN THERE, A CONSTRUCTION BOOM HAD TAKEN PLACE, HEIGHTENING AND BEAUTIFYING THE SKYLINE.

RAND THOUGHT THE CITY...

THE GREATEST MONUMENT TO THE POTENCY OF MAN'S MIND.

RAND'S FIRST NOVEL, 'WE THE LIVING' (1936), SHOWED THE SEVERITY OF LIFE IN COMMUNIST RUSSIA, ESPECIALLY FOR THE DESPISED MIDDLE CLASSES.

THE BOOK, WHICH IS SHOT THROUGH WITH AUTOBIOGRAPHICAL DETAILS, TELLS THE STORY OF THREE PEOPLE STRUGGLING UNDER SOVIET REPRESSION.

LIKE ALL RAND'S FICTION, 'WE THE LIVING' IS A ROMANTIC MELODRAMA WRAPPED IN PHILOSOPHICAL AND POLITICAL IDEAS.

IT DEMONSTRATES RAND'S BELIEF THAT ANY SYSTEM THAT REDUCED INDIVIDUAL RIGHTS FOR THE SAKE OF THE COMMON GOOD WOULD END IN DISASTER.

SHE BELIEVED THAT THE RIGHTS OF THE INDIVIDUAL WERE PARAMOUNT AND NOT TO BE INTERFERED WITH BY THE MAJORITY.

RAND PURSUED THIS THEME IN HER MOST FAMOUS NOVEL, 'THE FOUNTAINHEAD' (1943), A BOOK THAT WAS SEVEN YEARS IN THE WRITING.

'THE FOUNTAINHEAD' TELLS THE STORY OF THE ARCHITECT HOWARD ROARK, A KIND OF SUPER-INDIVIDUAL, WHO DEFIES THE CONVENTIONS OF THE WORLD AND DOES BATTLE WITH THE DULL CONFORMITY OF HIS PEERS.

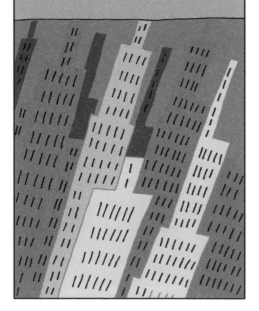

THE RUGGED, FLAME-HAIRED HERO IS HIRED TO DESIGN A HOUSING PROJECT FOR THE POOR, BUT ROARK DYNAMITES THE BUILDINGS WHEN HIS CLEAN-LINE MODERNIST PLANS ARE DEVIATED FROM.

AT HIS TRIAL, THE ARCHITECT DELIVERS A LONG SPEECH IN HIS OWN DEFENCE.

HE MAKES THE CASE THAT WITHOUT INDIVIDUAL CREATIVITY THERE WOULD BE NO SCIENTIFIC OR ARTISTIC PROGRESS.

MEDIOCRITY GENIUS

SUCH IDEAS ORIGINATE EXCLUSIVELY IN THE MIND OF MAN AND WILL BY THEIR VERY NEWNESS UPSET THE STATUS QUO.

ORIGINALITY ALWAYS ENGENDERS FEAR AND ENVY IN THOSE WHO PREFER CONFORMITY.

THE CREATIVE MAN OWES NOTHING TO THE REST OF HUMANITY, NOR DOES HE DEMAND ANYTHING IN RETURN.

ALL HE NEEDS IS TO BE TRUE TO HIMSELF AND HIS OWN IDEALS.

AT THE NOVEL'S HEART LIES RAND'S FEAR OF THE POWER OF THE COLLECTIVE OVER THE INDIVIDUAL.

IN HER VIEW, TO BE SELFLESS, TO WORK FOR ANOTHER'S BENEFIT, WAS TO BE A LESSER CREATURE.

RAND'S INTENTION IN CREATING THE CHARACTER OF HOWARD ROARK WAS TO SHOW WHAT A MAN COULD BE.

AT FIRST HE WOULD APPEAR MONSTROUSLY SELFISH.

BUT, BY THE END OF THE BOOK, READERS WOULD UNDERSTAND THAT SELFISHNESS, USUALLY THOUGHT OF AS A VICE, WAS IN FACT A VIRTUE...

WHILE ALTRUISM IS SHOWN TO BE MERELY A DEVICE USED TO ENSLAVE PEOPLE TO THE COLLECTIVE.

COLLECTIVISTS HUNGER FOR MEANING IN LIFE OUTSIDE OF THEIR OWN IDENTITY, THROUGH A BELIEF IN GOD, ALTRUISTIC PURPOSE, OR A DICTATOR WHO TELLS THEM WHAT TO DO.

I OBEY.

RAND REFERRED TO SUCH PEOPLE AS SECOND-HANDERS, BECAUSE THEY LIVED BY OTHER PEOPLE'S CHOICES AND NEEDED THE VALIDATION OF THE CROWD TO BOOST THEIR SELF-ESTEEM.

YOUR PAINTINGS ARE SIMPLY MARVELLOUS.

REALLY? I'LL HAVE TO DO MORE JUST LIKE THEM.

TRUE INDIVIDUALS LIVED BY THEIR OWN PRINCIPLES BASED ON THE ACTIONS OF THEIR OWN MINDS.

SECOND-HANDERS WERE PARASITES WHO USED THE LEVERS OF GOVERNMENT TO STEAL THE FRUITS OF AN INDIVIDUAL'S LABOUR.

TAXATION WAS THEFT AND THOSE WHO PERPETUATED THIS SYSTEM WERE NO MORE THAN LOOTERS. TRUE PROSPERITY AND FREEDOM COULD ONLY COME THROUGH AN UNRESTRAINED FREE MARKET.

RAND'S ELITIST VIEW WAS THAT THE MAJORITY OF PEOPLE FELL INTO THE INFERIOR SECOND-HANDER GROUP. THEY WERE PEOPLE WHO AVOIDED RESPONSIBILITY AND OWED ALL THE IMPROVEMENTS IN THEIR LIVES TO BETTER MEN.

IN HER WORLD, GOVERNMENT WOULD BE REDUCED TO THREE FUNCTIONS: THE ARMED SERVICES, THE POLICE, AND THE COURTS. INCOME TAXES WOULD END, ALONG WITH ALMOST EVERYTHING TAXES PAID FOR. ALL WELFARE BENEFITS WOULD BE REMOVED.

THE CREATOR'S CONCERN IS THE CONQUEST OF NATURE. THE PARASITE'S CONCERN IS THE CONQUEST OF MAN. IMPRESSED BY HOWARD ROARK'S ARGUMENT, THE JURY ACQUITS HIM.

NOT GUILTY.

THE NOVEL HAD MIXED REVIEWS AND A SLOW START IN TERMS OF SALES, BUT BY AUTUMN 1943 IT WAS CLEAR THAT THE BOOK WAS A BESTSELLER.

THE FOUNTAINHEAD

THE MOVIE RIGHTS WERE SOON SOLD, AND, AS A RESULT, RAND AND O'CONNOR MOVED BACK TO HOLLYWOOD SO THAT SHE COULD WRITE THE SCREENPLAY.

WHAT WAS MEANT TO BE A TEMPORARY STAY, FOR A FEW WEEKS, TURNED INTO YEARS.

RAND SECURED WORK DEVELOPING SCREENPLAYS AND THE COUPLE BOUGHT A HOUSE IN THE RURAL TOWN OF CHATSWORTH.

THE HOUSE WAS A SLEEK, MODERNIST, SWAN-SHAPED GLASS, STEEL AND CONCRETE STRUCTURE. A PLACE HOWARD ROARK HIMSELF WOULD HAVE BEEN PROUD TO DESIGN.

MARLENE DIETRICH LIVED HERE, YOU KNOW?

BACK THEN, HALF THE VALLEY WAS STILL COVERED IN ORANGE GROVES. FRANK FELL IN LOVE WITH THE PLACE.

HE GOT BUSY GROWING FRUIT TREES AND TENDING THE HOUSE'S EXPANSIVE GARDENS.

HE RAISED PEACOCKS, CHICKENS AND RABBITS, AND STARTED A BUSINESS SELLING GLADIOLI AND ALFALFA TO HOTELS.

RAND, WHO WAS OFTEN DEEP IN CONCENTRATION AT HER WORK, DIDN'T ALWAYS NOTICE FRANK'S COMINGS AND GOINGS.

SHE INSISTED THAT HE WEAR A SMALL BELL ON HIS SHOE, SO THAT SHE'D ALWAYS BE AWARE OF HIS PRESENCE.

FURTHER HUMILIATIONS WERE TO COME FOR POOR FRANK.

GARY COOPER PLAYED HOWARD ROARK IN THE 1949 FILM VERSION OF 'THE FOUNTAINHEAD', DIRECTED BY KING VIDOR. ALTHOUGH DRAMATICALLY SET AND BEAUTIFULLY SHOT, THE MOVIE IS A STIFF AFFAIR, STRIDENT AND JOYLESS.

IT'S A STRANGE MOVIE FOR HOLLYWOOD TO HAVE MADE, AND ITS POOR CRITICAL RECEPTION REFLECTED THIS. RAND INCREASINGLY DISLIKED THE FILM IN THE YEARS FOLLOWING, STATING THAT SHE WOULD NEVER AGAIN SELL ONE OF HER NOVELS TO A FILM COMPANY, UNLESS SHE HAD A RIGHT TO CHOOSE THE DIRECTOR AND SCREENWRITER, AND HAD CONTROL OVER THE EDITING.

AS THE BOOK CONTINUED TO SELL, RAND RECEIVED THOUSANDS OF FAN LETTERS. ONE WRITER IN PARTICULAR CAUGHT HER ATTENTION.

THIS WAS NATHAN BLUMENTHAL, A NINETEEN-YEAR-OLD COLLEGE FRESHMAN, WHO HAD READ 'THE FOUNTAINHEAD' FORTY TIMES SINCE HE WAS FOURTEEN.

IMPRESSED BY HIS INTELLIGENCE, RAND CORRESPONDED WITH THE YOUNG MAN, EVENTUALLY INVITING HIM TO THE CHATSWORTH RANCH.

THE TWO OF THEM TALKED FOR NINE AND A HALF HOURS. WHEN NATHAN LEFT IT WAS 5.30.

WHEN HE RETURNED TO CHATSWORTH, IT WAS IN THE COMPANY OF HIS GIRLFRIEND, BARBARA WEIDMAN.

IT SEEMED TO THE YOUNG COUPLE THAT THEY HAD WAITED ALL THEIR LIVES TO HEAR THE TRUTHS ONLY RAND COULD TELL THEM.

CAPITALISM IS THE ONLY ECONOMIC SYSTEM IN HISTORY TO OPERATE ON THE BASIS OF INDEPENDENT REASON.

WITHOUT CAPITALISM'S UNDERPINNINGS – THE RIGHT TO OWN PRIVATE PROPERTY AND TO WORK FOR ONE'S OWN PROFIT – NO OTHER POLITICAL RIGHTS CAN BE GUARANTEED.

IF THE STATE CAN SEIZE THE WEALTH AND PROPERTY A PERSON HAS ACQUIRED THROUGH HARD WORK, THEN WHY WOULD ANYONE INVENT ANYTHING NEW?

AS FRANK BECAME MORE INVOLVED IN HIS GARDENING PROJECTS AND MORE DISTANT FROM AYN...

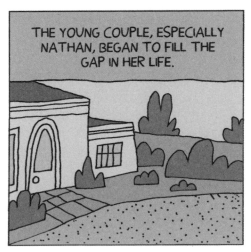

THE YOUNG COUPLE, ESPECIALLY NATHAN, BEGAN TO FILL THE GAP IN HER LIFE.

THEY WOULD VISIT RAND EVERY WEEKEND, AND THEN BY APPOINTMENT ON WEEKDAYS AND EVENINGS TOO.

BY THIS TIME RAND WAS HARD AT WORK ON HER LONGEST AND FINAL NOVEL.

ORIGINALLY KNOWN AS 'THE STRIKE', THE BOOK WOULD EVENTUALLY BE PUBLISHED UNDER THE TITLE 'ATLAS SHRUGGED'.

NATHAN AND BARBARA WERE THRILLED TO BE ABLE TO READ CHAPTERS OF THE NEW NOVEL AS RAND FINISHED THEM.

CHATSWORTH BECAME A REFUGE FOR THE TWO COLLEGE STUDENTS, WHOSE RIGHT-WING OPINIONS WERE UNPOPULAR AT THE UNIVERSITY OF CALIFORNIA...

WHILE FOR RAND, WHO HAD DIFFICULTY TOLERATING OPPOSING POINTS OF VIEW, THE YOUNG COUPLE WERE A PLEASURE.

RAND WAS THEIR IDOL. THEY HUNG ON HER EVERY WORD.

IN JUNE 1951 THIS TIGHT CIRCLE WAS BROKEN WHEN NATHAN AND BARBARA MOVED TO NEW YORK. BARBARA HAD ENROLLED IN A PHILOSOPHY MASTERS DEGREE COURSE AT NEW YORK UNIVERSITY. NATHAN WENT ALONG TO STUDY PSYCHOLOGY.

DEVASTATED, RAND CRIED ON THE DAY THEY LEFT.

SHE CONTINUED TO WORK ON HER NOVEL, REACHING THE LAST THIRD OF THE BOOK BY SEPTEMBER.

CLAIMING THAT SHE WAS TIRED OF CALIFORNIA AND THAT SHE NEEDED THE ENERGY OF NEW YORK TO FINISH THE BOOK, RAND CONVINCED FRANK THAT THEY MUST FOLLOW THE YOUNGER COUPLE.

O'CONNOR HAD LITTLE CHOICE. IT HAD BEEN OVER TWO DECADES SINCE HE HAD SUPPORTED HIMSELF FINANCIALLY. HE SAID A RELUCTANT GOODBYE TO HIS BELOVED GARDENS.

THE CHATSWORTH HOUSE WAS RENTED TO THEIR GOOD FRIENDS RUTH AND BUZZY HILL. FRANK EXPECTED TO BE AWAY FOR ONLY THE SHORT TIME IT WOULD TAKE FOR AYN TO COMPLETE THE NOVEL...

BUT THE HILLS WERE TO REMAIN TENANTS FOR TWENTY YEARS. FRANK WAS NEVER TO RETURN TO LIVE AT CHATSWORTH.

ONCE RAND WAS BACK IN NEW YORK, A SMALL CIRCLE OF PEOPLE BEGAN TO GATHER AROUND HER.

THIS GROUP WAS COMPOSED OF NATHAN, BARBARA, A FEW OF THEIR FRIENDS AND FAMILY, PLUS STUDENTS FROM THE UNIVERSITY.

WHAT ARE YOUR PRINCIPLES?

ER!

JOKINGLY CALLING THEMSELVES 'THE COLLECTIVE', THEY WERE DRAWN TOGETHER BY RAND'S STRONG PERSONALITY AND LITERARY FAME.

WELL?

ALL WERE YOUNG, PASSIONATE ABOUT IDEAS, AND EAGER TO HEAR THE WORDS OF THE SUCCESSFUL WRITER.

TO THINK FOR MYSELF. TO SEEK THE TRUTH NO MATTER WHERE IT MIGHT LEAD.

VERY GOOD.

ONE OF THESE EARLY RECRUITS WAS ALAN GREENSPAN, A FUTURE CHAIRMAN OF THE FEDERAL RESERVE BOARD.

BRIEFLY MARRIED TO BARBARA'S CLOSE FRIEND JOAN MITCHELL, GREENSPAN ENGAGED IN THE ALL-NIGHT DEBATES AND WROTE SPIRITED COMMENTARY FOR RAND'S NEWSLETTER.

GREENSPAN WAS BORN IN THE WASHINGTON HEIGHTS AREA OF NEW YORK IN 1926.

HIS PARENTS DIVORCED WHEN HE WAS FIVE YEARS OLD. HIS MOTHER TOOK HIM TO LIVE WITH HER OWN PARENTS IN THE BRONX.

AS A CHILD, HE SHOWED PRECOCIOUS INTELLIGENCE. HE WAS ABLE TO ADD UP THREE-DIGIT NUMBERS IN HIS HEAD.

DO IT AGAIN, ALAN.

THEY WERE A MUSICAL FAMILY. GREENSPAN TOOK UP THE CLARINET, SHARING A CLASS WITH STAN GETZ, AND LATER PLAYING IN THE WOODY HERMAN BAND.

DESCRIBED AS SOLITARY AND A STRAIGHT ARROW, GREENSPAN ASSERTED HIS INDEPENDENCE FROM HIS FAMILY BY REFUSING TO BE BAR-MITZVAHED.

I'M A SECULAR JEW.

HE STUDIED ECONOMICS AT NEW YORK UNIVERSITY, EARNING UNDERGRADUATE AND GRADUATE DEGREES IN THE SUBJECT.

CALLED 'THE UNDERTAKER' BY RAND, BECAUSE OF HIS QUIET AND SOMBRE NATURE, GREENSPAN NEVERTHELESS BECAME A FAVOURITE OF THE AUTHOR.

THE LIBERTARIAN ECONOMIST MURRAY ROTHBARD ALSO MET RAND AND HER COLLECTIVE AROUND THIS TIME.

RAND WAS NOT MY CUP OF TEA. SHE WAS EXHAUSTING. HER ENORMOUS HOPPED-UP ENERGY WAS OVERWHELMING.

I WAS HORRIFIED BY THE COLLECTIVE. THEY WERE A PASSIVE, DEPENDENT GROUP, WHO HOVERED AROUND RAND LIKE BEES.

THEY WERE ALMOST LIFELESS, DEVOID OF ENTHUSIASM OR SPARK, AND COMPLETELY DEPENDENT ON RAND FOR INTELLECTUAL SUSTENANCE.

I FELT THAT, IF I CONTINUED TO SEE HER, MY PERSONALITY AND INDEPENDENCE WOULD BECOME OVERWHELMED BY THE TREMENDOUS POWER OF HER WILL.

BARBARA WEIDMAN HAD LONG BEEN UNCERTAIN ABOUT HER FEELINGS FOR NATHAN.

WHEN SHE'D ENROLLED AT NEW YORK UNIVERSITY, SHE HAD ASSUMED THAT THE RELATIONSHIP WOULD END.

BUT NATHAN HAD TAGGED ALONG, AND THEN RAND HAD FOLLOWED.

ONE EVENING BARBARA FOUND HERSELF BEING QUESTIONED BY RAND ABOUT THE RELATIONSHIP.

SHE WAS FORCED TO ADMIT THAT SHE HAD SLEPT WITH ANOTHER MAN DURING THE SUMMER WHEN AWAY FROM NATHAN.

THAT BARBARA COULDN'T FULLY COMMIT TO NATHAN, WHO WAS CLEARLY HER INTELLECTUAL IDEAL, PROVED TO RAND THAT THE YOUNG WOMAN HAD PSYCHOLOGICAL PROBLEMS.

WITH RAND'S BLESSING, NATHAN THEN BECAME BARBARA'S UNOFFICIAL PSYCHOLOGIST.

AYN CONVINCED ME THAT NATHAN WAS AN EXCEPTIONAL MAN WITH A PROFOUND INTELLIGENCE. WE HAD ALL THE INGREDIENTS OF A SUCCESSFUL MARRIAGE.

THE COUPLE FINALLY MARRIED IN 1953...

CHANGING THEIR SURNAME TO BRANDEN (CHOSEN BECAUSE IT CONTAINED RAND). NATHAN BECAME NATHANIEL.

DURING THIS PERIOD, RAND WAS FORMULATING THE ESSENTIALS OF THE PHILOSOPHY SHE CALLED OBJECTIVISM.

MAN IS A RATIONAL CREATURE WHO USES HIS MIND TO SURVIVE.

THE RATIONAL FACULTY REQUIRES INDEPENDENCE AND INDIVIDUALITY TO OPERATE PROPERLY.

THEREFORE AN ETHICS OF SELFISHNESS IS APPROPRIATE FOR RATIONAL MAN.

ANY MORAL AND ETHICAL PROBLEM CAN BE APPROACHED FROM THIS PERSPECTIVE.

RAND PLACED THESE VALUES AT THE HEART OF HER MAGNUM OPUS, 'ATLAS SHRUGGED'.

WHAT IF THE CREATIVE PEOPLE OF THE WORLD, THE PRIME MOVERS, REFUSED TO ALLOW THEIR INVENTIONS, ART, BUSINESS LEADERSHIP, SCIENTIFIC RESEARCH, OR ANY NEW IDEAS TO BE USED BY GOVERNMENT? WHAT IF THEY REFUSED TO HAVE THEIR WEALTH STOLEN FROM THEM IN TAXATION AND WITHDREW THEIR LABOUR? WHAT IF THEY WENT ON STRIKE?

THE NOVEL TELLS THE APOCALYPTIC TALE OF AN AMERICA RUINED BY COLLECTIVISM, WHERE INDUSTRIALISTS ARE PUBLICLY DERIDED FOR GETTING RICH AT THE EXPENSE OF THE POOR, AND WHERE PROFITS ARE APPROPRIATED FOR THE SAKE OF THE PEOPLE. IN THIS WORLD MEDIOCRITY IS THE GOAL, AND HIGH ACHIEVERS ARE THE ENEMY.

YET AT A TIME OF CRISIS, WHEN THEY ARE MOST NEEDED, THE COUNTRY'S TOP INDUSTRIALISTS ARE VANISHING, LEAVING THEIR BANKS, MINES, AND FACTORIES WITHOUT LEADERSHIP. THE INCOMPETENT SECOND-HANDERS WHO ARE LEFT IN CHARGE CAN ONLY WATCH HELPLESSLY AS INDUSTRY SHUTS DOWN AND AMERICA BEGINS TO RUN OUT OF COAL, STEEL, AND MANUFACTURING GOODS.

THE MYSTERIOUS FIGURE AT THE HEART OF THE NOVEL IS THE COPPER-HAIRED HEROIC GENIUS JOHN GALT.

IT IS GALT, THE STORY REVEALS, WHO HAS LURED THESE TITANS OF INDUSTRY TO HIS SECRET MOUNTAIN TOWN OF GALT'S GULCH, COLORADO, WHERE TOGETHER THEY HAVE CREATED A UTOPIAN FREE MARKET.

'ATLAS SHRUGGED' FINISHES AS 'THE FOUNTAINHEAD' DOES, WITH A LONG SPEECH, AS JOHN GALT BROADCASTS HIS MANIFESTO TO A DYING AMERICA...

A SPEECH THAT ENDS WITH GALT PROMISING THAT THE STRIKERS WOULD SOON RETURN TO RESCUE A CRUMBLING WORLD.

TWELVE YEARS IN THE WRITING, 'ATLAS SHRUGGED' WAS PUBLISHED ON OCTOBER 10, 1957. THE REVIEWS WERE SCATHING.

COVER BY FRANK O'CONNOR.

IT WOULD BE HARD TO FIND ANOTHER SUCH DISPLAY OF GROTESQUE ECCENTRICITY OUTSIDE OF AN INSANE ASYLUM. JOHN GALT IS REALLY ARGUING FOR A DICTATORSHIP.

ROBERT KIRSCH, 'LOS ANGELES TIMES'.

FROM ALMOST ANY PAGE OF 'ATLAS SHRUGGED', A VOICE CAN BE HEARD, COMMANDING, 'TO A GAS CHAMBER – GO!'

WHITTAKER CHAMBERS, 'NATIONAL REVIEW'.

RAND HAD EXPECTED TO BE ATTACKED, BUT SHE HADN'T THOUGHT HER WORLD VIEW WOULD BE COMPARED TO FASCISM.

POST PUBLICATION OF THE BOOK, SHE FELL INTO A DEEP DEPRESSION.

SALES WERE STRONG, BUT THIS WAS NOT ENOUGH FOR RAND, WHO HAD BELIEVED THE NOVEL WOULD BE HAILED AS A MAJOR WORK THAT WOULD PROFOUNDLY CHANGE THE AMERICAN POLITICAL SCENE.

OWING TO THEIR CLOSENESS AND MUTUAL INTERESTS, PERHAPS IT WAS INEVITABLE THAT AYN AND NATHANIEL'S FRIENDSHIP WOULD DEVELOP INTO SOMETHING MORE.

NATHANIEL COULD OFFER RAND WHAT HER PASSIVE HUSBAND COULD NOT: INTELLECTUAL STIMULATION AND EMOTIONAL SUPPORT.

THE AFFAIR HAD BEGUN IN 1954 WHEN HE HAD BEEN TWENTY-FIVE AND SHE'D BEEN FORTY-NINE.

AYN!

NATHANIEL!

THEY DID NOT ATTEMPT TO HIDE THE RELATIONSHIP FROM THEIR SPOUSES. IN A MEETING THE FOUR OF THEM HAD, RAND CONVINCED FRANK AND BARBARA THAT ALLOWING THE AFFAIR WOULD BE THE HONEST AND RATIONAL THING TO DO.

WE ARE SUPERIOR PEOPLE, WHO NEED A SUPERIOR SOLUTION.

WITH AYN'S MIND, ONCE YOU ACCEPTED HER PREMISES, SHE'D SPIN A DEDUCTIVE CHAIN FROM WHICH YOU JUST COULDN'T ESCAPE.

NATHANIEL SUGGESTED THAT THEY SHOULD RENT A SMALL APARTMENT WHERE THE TWO OF THEM COULD MEET.

AYN WAS AGAINST THIS IDEA, FEARING THAT NEWS OF THE AFFAIR WOULD LEAK BEYOND THE FOUR OF THEM...

SO IT WAS AGREED THAT NATHANIEL WOULD MEET AYN TWICE A WEEK AT HER APARTMENT.

THIS MUST HAVE BEEN ESPECIALLY DIFFICULT FOR FRANK, WHO WAS DISPLACED FROM HIS OWN HOME FOR THE DURATION OF THE TRYST.

HIS DESTINATION WAS OFTEN A LOCAL BAR.

BARBARA BEGAN TO HAVE ANXIETY ATTACKS AND FAINTING FITS.

UGH!

THE ADULTEROUS COUPLE WERE OBLIVIOUS TO THE CAUSE OF THESE SYMPTOMS.

SHE'S SUCH AN EMOTIONALIST.

WHEN NATHANIEL TOOK HIS MASTER'S DEGREE IN PSYCHOLOGY, HE WROTE HIS THESIS ON ANXIETY AND SELF-ESTEEM.

SOB!

IT SEEMS LIKELY THAT HIS INTEREST IN THIS AREA CAME OUT OF THE LONG THERAPEUTIC SESSIONS HE CONDUCTED WITH HIS WIFE.

CHARISMATIC AND CONFIDENT, NATHANIEL BECAME RAND'S PUBLIC FACE, PROMOTING HER VIEWS AND VIGOROUSLY DEFENDING HER FROM ATTACK.

WITH HER PERMISSION, HE STARTED A LECTURE SERIES, OUTLINING THE PRINCIPLES OF OBJECTIVISM.

RAND DIDN'T WANT HER NAME DIRECTLY CONNECTED WITH THE LECTURES. SHE FEARED OTHER PEOPLE'S ERRORS BEING ATTRIBUTED TO HER.

AND SO THE NATHANIEL BRANDEN INSTITUTE (NBI) WAS BORN.

HOWEVER, RAND DID SPEAK AT THESE EARLY LECTURES, AS DID ALAN GREENSPAN.

IT PROVED A MONEY-SPINNING IDEA. THE CONCEPT WAS SOON EXPANDED TO THE SELLING OF TAPED LECTURES.

THESE TAPES WOULD BE SENT TO APPROVED REPRESENTATIVES ACROSS THE COUNTRY.

IT'S HERE!

GOSH!

EAGER STUDENTS WOULD THEN PAY TO LISTEN TO NATHANIEL'S TWENTY-WEEK LECTURE SERIES.

BLAH, BLAH, BLAH, BLAH, BLAH!

AS THE NBI BECAME A LUCRATIVE BUSINESS, NATHANIEL WAS ABLE TO LEASE OFFICES IN THE EMPIRE STATE BUILDING...

ALTHOUGH THEY WERE UNHEROICALLY LOCATED IN THE BASEMENT.

IT'S A LITTLE DARK DOWN HERE.

RAND'S GRIP ON THE MOVEMENT REMAINED ABSOLUTE.

MEMBERS OF THE COLLECTIVE WHO DISPLEASED HER RISKED EXCOMMUNICATION.

WHAT DID YOU SAY?

UH...

PERCEIVED DEVIATION FROM THE OBJECTIVIST LINE WOULD ENGENDER EXCRUCIATING PERSONAL INTERROGATION AT ONE OF RAND'S APARTMENT GATHERINGS. EVENTS THAT WERE BASICALLY TRIALS.

NATHANIEL WOULD EVENTUALLY WRITE ABOUT THIS PERIOD.

WE WERE NOT A CULT IN THE LITERAL DICTIONARY SENSE OF THE WORD...

BUT THERE WAS A CULTISH ASPECT TO OUR WORLD. WE WERE A GROUP ORGANISED AROUND A CHARISMATIC LEADER...

WHOSE MEMBERS JUDGED ONE ANOTHER'S CHARACTERS BY THE LOYALTY TO THAT LEADER AND HER IDEAS.

RAND'S PHILOSOPHY SAW ALL OF REALITY INTEGRATED BY A FEW FUNDAMENTAL PRINCIPLES. THESE PRINCIPLES COULD BE SEEN IN ALL ASPECTS OF A PERSON'S LIFE.

THEREFORE IT WAS POSSIBLE TO GAUGE AN OBJECTIVIST'S COMMITMENT BY LOOKING AT THE SMALLEST DETAIL OF HIS OR HER LIFE.

AN OBJECTIVIST WAS EXPECTED TO BE JUDGED ON EVERYTHING, AND, IN TURN, THEY WERE EXPECTED TO JUDGE OTHERS. IT WAS THE PERFECT BREEDING GROUND FOR FEAR AND PARANOIA.

YEARS EARLIER, MURRAY ROTHBARD HAD SEEN THE FATAL FLAW IN RAND'S PHILOSOPHY.

THE FAMOUS INDIVIDUALIST ACTUALLY DENIES ALL INDIVIDUALITY WHATSOEVER.

A RANDIAN UTOPIA WOULD BE A PLACE WHERE ALL MEN ARE IDENTICAL, IN THEIR SOULS, IF NOT IN THEIR PERSONAL APPEARANCE.

BY THE EARLY 1960s, RAND AND THE BRANDENS WERE LINKED THROUGH MULTIPLE BUSINESS AND CREATIVE VENTURES.

BOTH COUPLES MOVED INTO APARTMENTS IN THE SAME NEWLY BUILT HIGH-RISE IN MANHATTAN.

THE SCENE WAS SET FOR DISASTER.

O'CONNOR USED A ONE-ROOM APARTMENT IN THE BUILDING AS AN ART STUDIO.

FRANK SHOWED SOME TALENT, BUT RAND WOULDNT ALLOW HIM TO SELL ANY OF HIS PAINTINGS.

I COULDN'T BEAR TO PART WITH ANY OF THEM.

ANOTHER SET OF ROOMS WAS TURNED BY BARBARA INTO OFFICES FOR THE NBI AND 'THE OBJECTIVIST NEWSLETTER'...

WHILE NATHANIEL HAD AN OFFICE IN THE BRANDENS' OWN APARTMENT, WHERE HE CONDUCTED THERAPY SESSIONS.

HE'D DEVELOPED A THRIVING PSYCHOTHERAPEUTIC CAREER OFF THE BACK OF HIS NBI LECTURES.

IN LATE 1963, NATHANIEL BEGAN AN AFFAIR WITH ONE OF HIS PATIENTS.

PATRECIA GULLISON WAS A TWENTY-FIVE-YEAR-OLD MODEL WHOM NATHANIEL HAD MET TWO YEARS EARLIER AFTER SHE HAD ENROLLED IN HIS LECTURE SERIES.

IN 1962, PATRECIA MARRIED ANOTHER NBI REGULAR, LARRY SCOTT.

BOTH THE O'CONNORS AND THE BRANDENS ATTENDED THE WEDDING.

WHEN THE NEWLYWEDS LET IT BE KNOWN THAT THEY WERE HAVING MARITAL PROBLEMS, NATHANIEL OFFERED TO GIVE THEM FREE MARRIAGE COUNSELLING.

THE AFFAIR BEGAN SHORTLY AFTER THIS.

BY THIS TIME, BARBARA HAD RENEWED A RELATIONSHIP WITH AN OLD FLAME. SHE WAS HONEST WITH NATHANIEL AND SOUGHT HIS PERMISSION TO SEE THIS OTHER MAN.

DO AS YOU WANT.

BARBARA SUSPECTED THAT NATHANIEL WAS ALSO HAVING AN AFFAIR, BUT HE DENIED IT SO STRONGLY THAT SHE DOUBTED HER OWN SENSES.

YOU'RE PARANOID.

THE TRUTH WAS THAT NATHANIEL WAS TERRIFIED THAT RAND WOULD FIND OUT ABOUT GULLISON.

HE'D BUILT A CAREER OUT OF HIS CONNECTION WITH AYN. ANY RIFT WITH HER MIGHT PROVE FINANCIALLY DISASTROUS FOR HIM.

HIS RELATIONSHIP WITH RAND HAD BEEN PLATONIC FOR SOME YEARS...

BUT SHE HAD RECENTLY BEEN PRESSURING HIM FOR A RESUMPTION OF THEIR ROMANCE.

AM I TOO OLD FOR YOU? AM I NOT SEXUALLY ATTRACTIVE?

I DON'T KNOW.

YOU DON'T KNOW?

MEANWHILE, IT WAS THE...

1960s

AND THE WORLD HAD CHANGED

STOP THE WAR

UNLIKE THE MAJORITY OF THOSE ON THE RIGHT, RAND OPPOSED THE VIETNAM WAR.

SHE WAS ALSO AGAINST THE DRAFT, WHICH SHE SAW AS A VIOLATION OF INDIVIDUAL RIGHTS. THE STATE SHOULD NOT HAVE THE POWER TO SEND MEN TO THEIR DEATHS.

FOR SIMILAR REASONS, SHE SPOKE OUT AGAINST STATE GOVERNMENTS' BANS ON ABORTION.

ABORTION IS A MORAL RIGHT, WHICH SHOULD BE LEFT TO THE SOLE DISCRETION OF THE WOMAN.

IN A POLITICAL RIGHT DOMINATED BY RELIGION, RAND WAS FURTHER ALIENATED FROM THEM BY HER ATHEISM.

THERE IS NO GOD.

YET IN OTHER WAYS SHE REMAINED DEEPLY CONSERVATIVE.

THE FEMINIST MOVEMENT IS UTTERLY WITHOUT LEGITIMACY.

RAND THOUGHT FEMINISM TO BE MERELY ANOTHER FORM OF COLLECTIVISM...

SHE WHAT?

AN INVENTED OPPRESSED CLASS THAT LOOKED TO GOVERNMENT TO REDRESS DISCRIMINATION THAT WAS CAUSED BY WOMEN THEMSELVES IN THE FIRST PLACE.

TRAITOR!

THE NOTION THAT A WOMAN'S PLACE IS IN THE HOME IS AN ANCIENT, PRIMITIVE EVIL, PERPETUATED BY WOMEN, AS MUCH AS OR MORE THAN BY MEN.

SHE ATTACKED NATIVE AMERICANS, REFERRING TO THEM AS SAVAGES.

IN HER VIEW, THE SUPERIOR TECHNOLOGICAL CULTURE WILL ALWAYS PREVAIL AGAINST AN INFERIOR, LESS DEVELOPED ONE. THE TRIBES THAT OCCUPIED THE LAND FOR THOUSANDS OF YEARS HAD DONE NOTHING WITH IT, AND SHOULD STAND ASIDE FOR THOSE WHO WOULD.

IN 1967, WHEN FRANK TURNED SEVENTY, HE BEGAN SUFFERING PAINFUL CONTRACTIONS IN HIS HANDS.

OUCH!

THIS PROBLEM LED TO HIM HAVING TO GIVE UP PAINTING, AS HE COULD NO LONGER HOLD THE BRUSHES AND COMPLETE THE FINE DETAIL HE NEEDED.

SIGH!

HE STILL KEPT UP THE STUDIO, BUT IT IS CLAIMED BY SOME, THAT HE WAS USING IT AS A PLACE TO DRINK.

THE BRANDENS SEPARATED, THEN DIVORCED, SENDING SHOCKWAVES THROUGH THE OBJECTIVIST MOVEMENT.

RAND SAW THIS AS AN OPPORTUNITY FOR NATHANIEL TO RETURN TO HER.

NOW WE CAN BE TOGETHER AGAIN.

NATHANIEL CHOSE TO SEND RAND A LETTER RATHER THAN FACE HER IN PERSON, EXPLAINING THAT THE DIFFERENCE IN THEIR AGES WAS A 'BARRIER TO HIS SEXUAL RESPONSE'.

WHAT?

THE STRAINED RELATIONSHIPS WITHIN THE COLLECTIVE LIMPED ALONG FOR A FEW MORE MONTHS.

THEN BARBARA, WORRIED ABOUT HER EX-HUSBAND'S HEALTH, BLEW THE WHISTLE.

NATHANIEL LOOKED HAGGARD AND SICKLY, AND SHE HERSELF WAS TIRED OF THE LIES AND HALF-TRUTHS THEY WERE LIVING WITH.

IT'S LONG PAST THE TIME WE TOLD HER.

GO TELL HER, THEN.

SO, WHILE NATHANIEL COWERED IN HIS APARTMENT, BARBARA TOOK THE ELEVATOR DOWN TO SEE THE FIRST LADY OF LOGIC.

THEN SHE EXPLAINED IT ALL.

SHE TOLD AYN THAT NATHANIEL HAD BEEN HAVING AN AFFAIR WITH GULLISON FOR FOUR AND HALF YEARS.

I'VE KNOWN ABOUT IT MYSELF FOR TWO YEARS, BUT I DIDN'T KNOW UNTIL RECENTLY HOW LONG THE AFFAIR HAD BEEN GOING ON.

GET THAT BASTARD DOWN HERE OR I'LL DRAG HIM DOWN HERE MYSELF!

RING! RING!

SHE WANTS TO SEE YOU, RIGHT NOW!

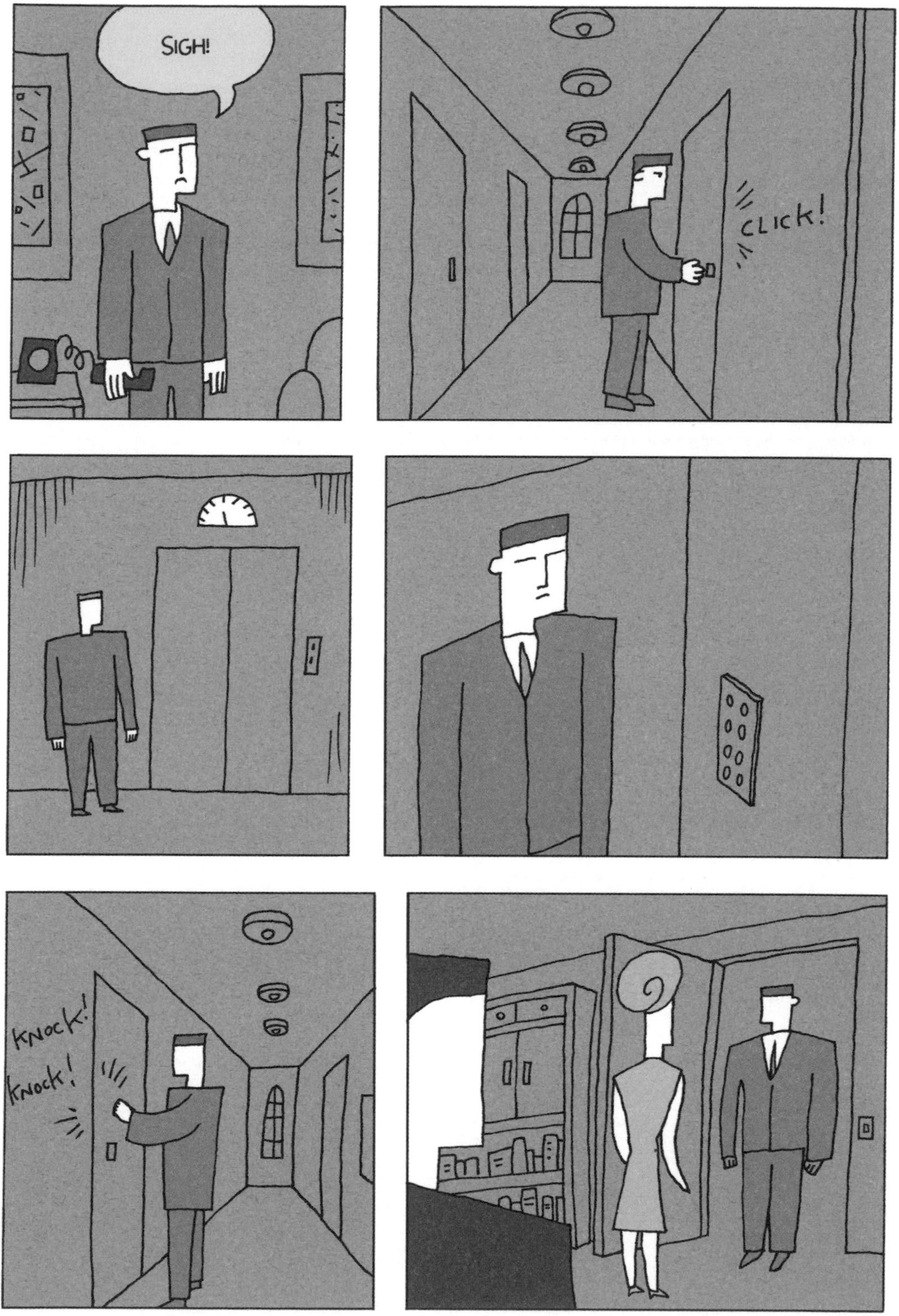
SIGH!
CLICK!
KNOCK!
KNOCK!

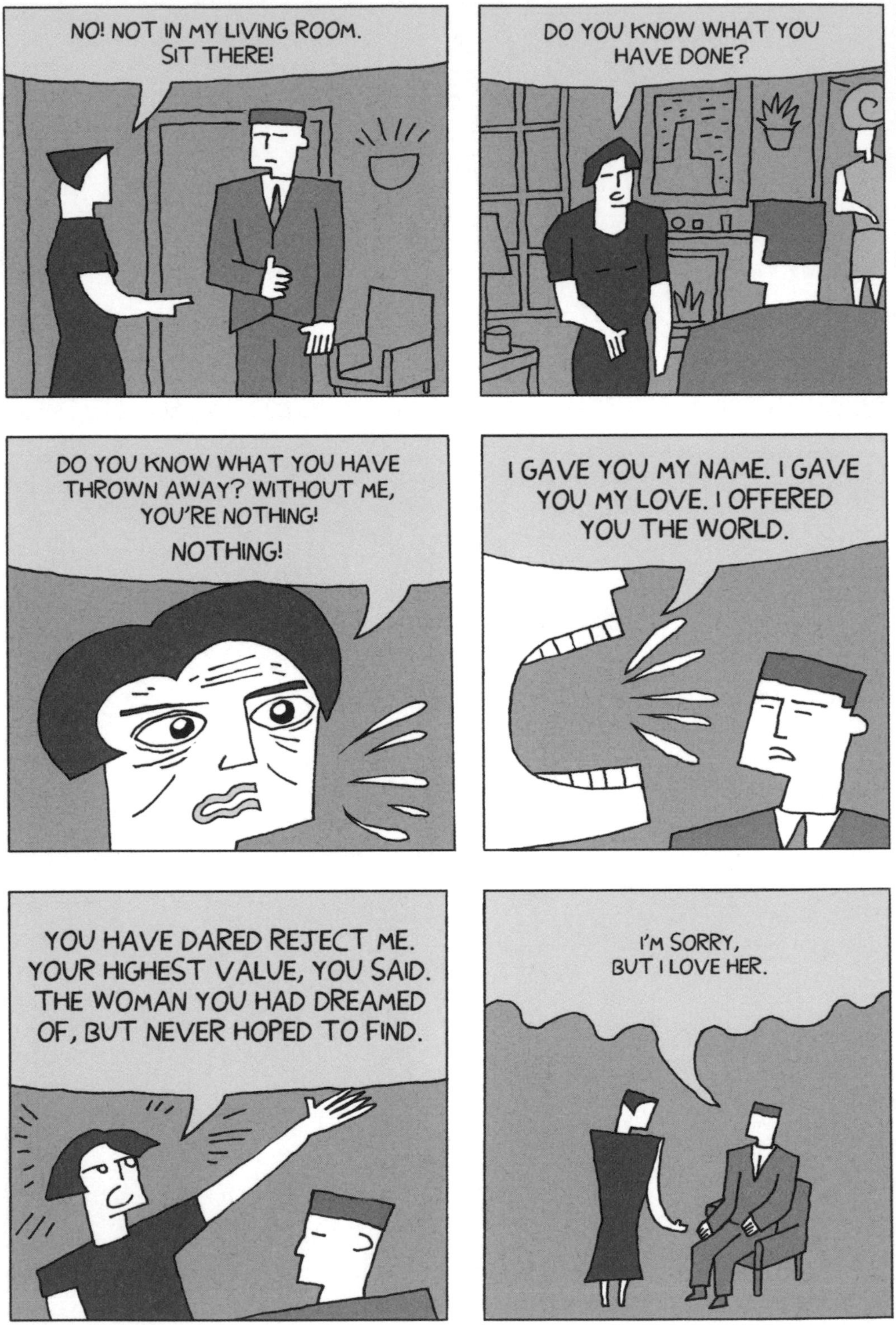
NO! NOT IN MY LIVING ROOM.
SIT THERE!
DO YOU KNOW WHAT YOU
HAVE DONE?
DO YOU KNOW WHAT YOU HAVE
THROWN AWAY? WITHOUT ME,
YOU'RE NOTHING!
NOTHING!
I GAVE YOU MY NAME. I GAVE
YOU MY LOVE. I OFFERED
YOU THE WORLD.
YOU HAVE DARED REJECT ME.
YOUR HIGHEST VALUE, YOU SAID.
THE WOMAN YOU HAD DREAMED
OF, BUT NEVER HOPED TO FIND.
I'M SORRY,
BUT I LOVE HER.

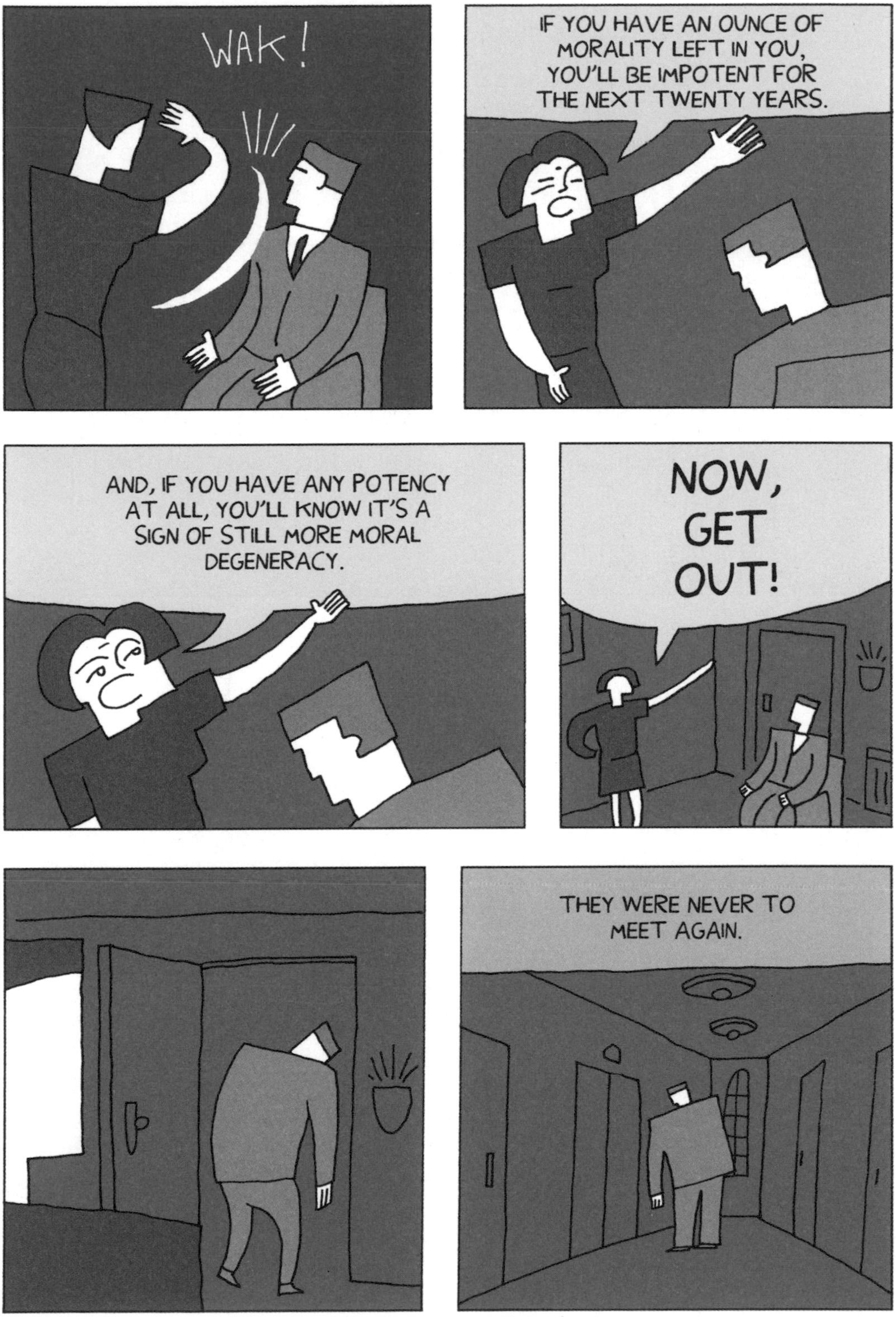
WAK!
IF YOU HAVE AN OUNCE OF MORALITY LEFT IN YOU, YOU'LL BE IMPOTENT FOR THE NEXT TWENTY YEARS.
AND, IF YOU HAVE ANY POTENCY AT ALL, YOU'LL KNOW IT'S A SIGN OF STILL MORE MORAL DEGENERACY.
NOW, GET OUT!
THEY WERE NEVER TO MEET AGAIN.

NATHANIEL HAD BECOME WEALTHY THROUGH HIS CONNECTION WITH RAND. THE NBI HAD BECOME A NATIONAL INSTITUTION. HE WAS THE PUBLIC FACE OF OBJECTIVISM, AN ADMIRED LEADER AND RAND'S CHOSEN HEIR. ALL THIS WAS NOW OVER.

RAND QUICKLY DISMANTLED THE NBI AND SEVERED ALL BUSINESS CONNECTIONS WITH NATHANIEL. SHE ATTACKED HIM IN THE PAGES OF 'THE OBJECTIVIST' MAGAZINE, ACCUSING HER ONE-TIME PROTÉGÉ OF FINANCIAL MISDEEDS AND UNSPECIFIED DECEPTIONS. WHAT SHE FAILED TO TELL WAS THE TRUTH.

BARBARA WAS ALSO TO SUFFER THE CONSEQUENCES OF RAND'S ANGER.

I'M VERY CONCERNED ABOUT AYN'S DETERIORATING MENTAL HEALTH AND RECKLESS BEHAVIOUR.

SHE THINKS YOU'RE LOSING YOUR MIND.

WHAT?

I WANT TO SEE HER.

BARBARA KNEW WHAT THIS MEANT AND REFUSED TO GO.

NO.

IN HER ABSENCE, SHE WAS FOUND GUILTY OF MAKING FALSE AND IMMORAL STATEMENTS.

SO THAT WAS IT. AFTER NINETEEN YEARS OF ALMOST DAILY CONTACT, I FOUND MYSELF SUDDENLY DISMISSED. I WAS TO SEE AYN ONLY ONCE MORE BEFORE SHE DIED.

NATHANIEL MOVED TO CALIFORNIA, WHERE HE AND PATRECIA WERE MARRIED IN NOVEMBER 1969.

PATRECIA DIED IN A DROWNING ACCIDENT IN 1977.

ALTHOUGH STILL SUPPORTIVE OF THE GENERAL OUTLINES OF OBJECTIVISM, NATHANIEL WAS EVENTUALLY TO CRITICISE CERTAIN ASPECTS OF RAND'S PHILOSOPHY.

IN PARTICULAR, IT WAS THE WAY SHE ENCOURAGED EMOTIONAL REPRESSION AND HER FAILURE TO APPRECIATE THE IMPORTANCE OF KINDNESS IN HUMAN RELATIONS.

RAND'S TENDENCY TO SHED FRIENDS AND FOLLOWERS THROUGH VARIOUS PURGES CONTINUED INTO HER OLD AGE.

AMONG THE FEW WHO WHO REMAINED CONSTANT WAS ALAN GREENSPAN.

IN JULY 1969, GREENSPAN ARRANGED FOR RAND TO WITNESS THE LAUNCH OF APOLLO 11 AT CAPE KENNEDY, FLORIDA.

THE EVENT THRILLED HER, EVEN THOUGH SHE DIDN'T APPROVE OF GOVERNMENT-FUNDED SCIENCE PROJECTS, UNLESS THEY WERE OF A MILITARY NATURE.

THOSE WHO SUGGEST WE SUBSTITUTE A WAR ON POVERTY FOR THE SPACE PROGRAMME SHOULD ASK THEMSELVES...

WHETHER THE PREMISES AND VALUES THAT FORM THE CHARACTER OF AN ASTRONAUT WOULD BE SATISFIED BY A LIFETIME OF CARRYING BEDPANS...

AND TEACHING THE ALPHABET TO THE MENTALLY RETARDED?

IN 1974, GREENSPAN WAS MADE CHAIRMAN OF PRESIDENT GERALD FORD'S COUNCIL OF ECONOMIC ADVISERS.

RAND, WITH FRANK IN TOW, TRAVELLED TO WASHINGTON FOR GREENSPAN'S SWEARING-IN.

AYN BROADENED MY HORIZONS FAR BEYOND THE MODEL OF ECONOMICS I HAD LEARNED. I'M GRATEFUL FOR THE INFLUENCE SHE HAD ON MY LIFE.

IN THE MID-1970s, FRANK BEGAN TO SHOW SYMPTOMS OF DEMENTIA.

YOU HAVE YOUR SHIRT ON BACKWARDS.

THIS WOULDN'T HAVE BEEN HELPED BY HIS CONTINUED DRINKING.

RAND, TYPICALLY, DID NOT UNDERSTAND WHAT HER HUSBAND WAS EXPERIENCING, OR THE ILLNESS ITSELF.

YOU'VE WET YOURSELF.

SHE WOULD GIVE HIM LONG, GRUELLING LESSONS ON HOW TO THINK AND REMEMBER.

YOU HAVEN'T FINISHED IT.

I CAN'T.

AS THE DISEASE PROGRESSED, O'CONNOR BECAME FRAIL AND HOUSEBOUND.

DON'T LEAVE ME, FRANK.

RAND ALSO SUFFERED HEALTH PROBLEMS.

SHE WAS CONSTANTLY TIRED AND SHORT OF BREATH.

WHEEZE!

BUT SHE WOULD NOT STOP HER HEAVY SMOKING. SHE DERIDED THE ANTI-SMOKING LOBBY AS ABSURD.

THERE IS NO CONNECTION BETWEEN SMOKING AND ILL HEALTH.

GIVE ME ONE RATIONAL REASON WHY I SHOULD NOT SMOKE.

RAND'S DOCTOR GAVE HER A REASON.

YOU HAVE LUNG CANCER.

SHE HAD ONE LUNG REMOVED AND REMAINED IN HOSPITAL FOR NEARLY A MONTH.

BAH!

SHE QUIT SMOKING, BUT REFUSED TO MAKE THIS DECISION PUBLIC.

I STILL THINK THERE IS NO CONNECTION BETWEEN SMOKING AND ILL HEALTH.

MUCH HAS BEEN MADE OF THE FACT THAT RAND SOUGHT AND RECEIVED SOCIAL SECURITY TOWARDS THE END OF HER LIFE.

SHE IS ACCUSED OF HYPOCRISY, OF BEING ONE OF THE VERY MOOCHERS AND TAKERS SHE SO DESPISED.

BUT IT WAS HER VIEW THAT THIS WAS A SYSTEM SHE HAD PAID INTO AGAINST HER WILL...

AND THAT SHE WAS MERELY TAKING BACK WHAT WAS HERS TO BEGIN WITH.

IN OTHER WORDS, IT IS EXACTLY WHAT THE MAJORITY OF PEOPLE DO WHEN THEY APPLY FOR SOCIAL SECURITY OR ANY OTHER WELFARE BENEFIT. YET RAND STILL THOUGHT HERSELF SUPERIOR TO THE MASSES SHE SAW ALL AROUND HER.

RAND'S LIFE WAS FULL OF SUCH CONTRADICTIONS. HER NOVELS WERE HIGH-MINDED AND PHILOSOPHICAL, YET ALSO FULL OF SOAP OPERA TRASHINESS, OVERWROUGHT EMOTIONS AND THIN CHARACTERISATIONS.

SHE TRUMPETED THE VIRTUE OF REASON OVER EMOTION, BUT WAS UNABLE TO RISE ABOVE JEALOUSY AND WAS UNFORGIVING TOWARDS ANYONE SHE BELIEVED HAD SLIGHTED HER.

SHE UPHELD AN INDIVIDUAL'S FREEDOM ABOVE ALL ELSE, YET RAN HER IMMEDIATE CIRCLE OF FRIENDS LIKE A SMALL DICTATORSHIP, WHERE OPPOSING VIEWS WERE NOT ALLOWED AND WHERE DISSENT WAS PUNISHED WITH EXPULSION.

SHE PRIDED HERSELF ON HER LOGIC AND THE ABILITY OF HER SENSES TO DISCOVER THE TRUTH OF THE WORLD. YET SHE FAILED TO SEE THROUGH HER LOVER'S DECEIT, EVEN THOUGH THE EVIDENCE HAD BEEN IN FRONT OF HER FOR YEARS.

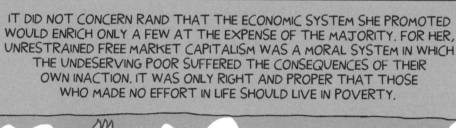

IT DID NOT CONCERN RAND THAT THE ECONOMIC SYSTEM SHE PROMOTED WOULD ENRICH ONLY A FEW AT THE EXPENSE OF THE MAJORITY. FOR HER, UNRESTRAINED FREE MARKET CAPITALISM WAS A MORAL SYSTEM IN WHICH THE UNDESERVING POOR SUFFERED THE CONSEQUENCES OF THEIR OWN INACTION. IT WAS ONLY RIGHT AND PROPER THAT THOSE WHO MADE NO EFFORT IN LIFE SHOULD LIVE IN POVERTY.

AFTER RAND'S DEATH, HER IDEAS WERE TAKEN UP BY A BROADER AUDIENCE OF LIBERTARIANS, WHO THEN INJECTED HER FREE MARKET IDEOLOGY INTO THE POLITICAL MAINSTREAM. A GROWING NUMBER OF RIGHT- WING THINK TANKS, SUCH AS THE CATO INSTITUTE, WOULD THROUGHOUT THE 1970s REFASHION THE POLITICAL CONSENSUS AROUND THE DESIRABILITY OF UNREGULATED CAPITALISM.

SELFISHNESS EXISTED LONG BEFORE AYN RAND. HER VIEWPOINT WAS HARDLY NOVEL, BUT, FOR THOSE ON THE POLITICAL RIGHT, THE NEW ELEMENT SHE BROUGHT TO THE DISCUSSION WAS A PHILOSOPHICAL AND MORAL JUSTIFICATION FOR THEIR ACTIONS. WITH RAND AS THEIR GODDESS, THEY COULD LIVE GUILT- FREE WITH THEIR INDIFFERENCE TO THOSE WITH FEWER OPPORTUNITIES THAN THEMSELVES.

AYN RAND DIED ON MARCH 6, 1982, AFTER A BOUT OF PNEUMONIA.

HUNDREDS QUEUED OUTSIDE THE MADISON AVENUE FUNERAL HOME FOR THEIR LAST CHANCE TO SEE HER.

NEXT TO HER COFFIN STOOD THE SYMBOL OF HER LIFE...

A SIX-FOOT-HIGH FLORAL DESIGN IN THE SHAPE OF THE US DOLLAR.

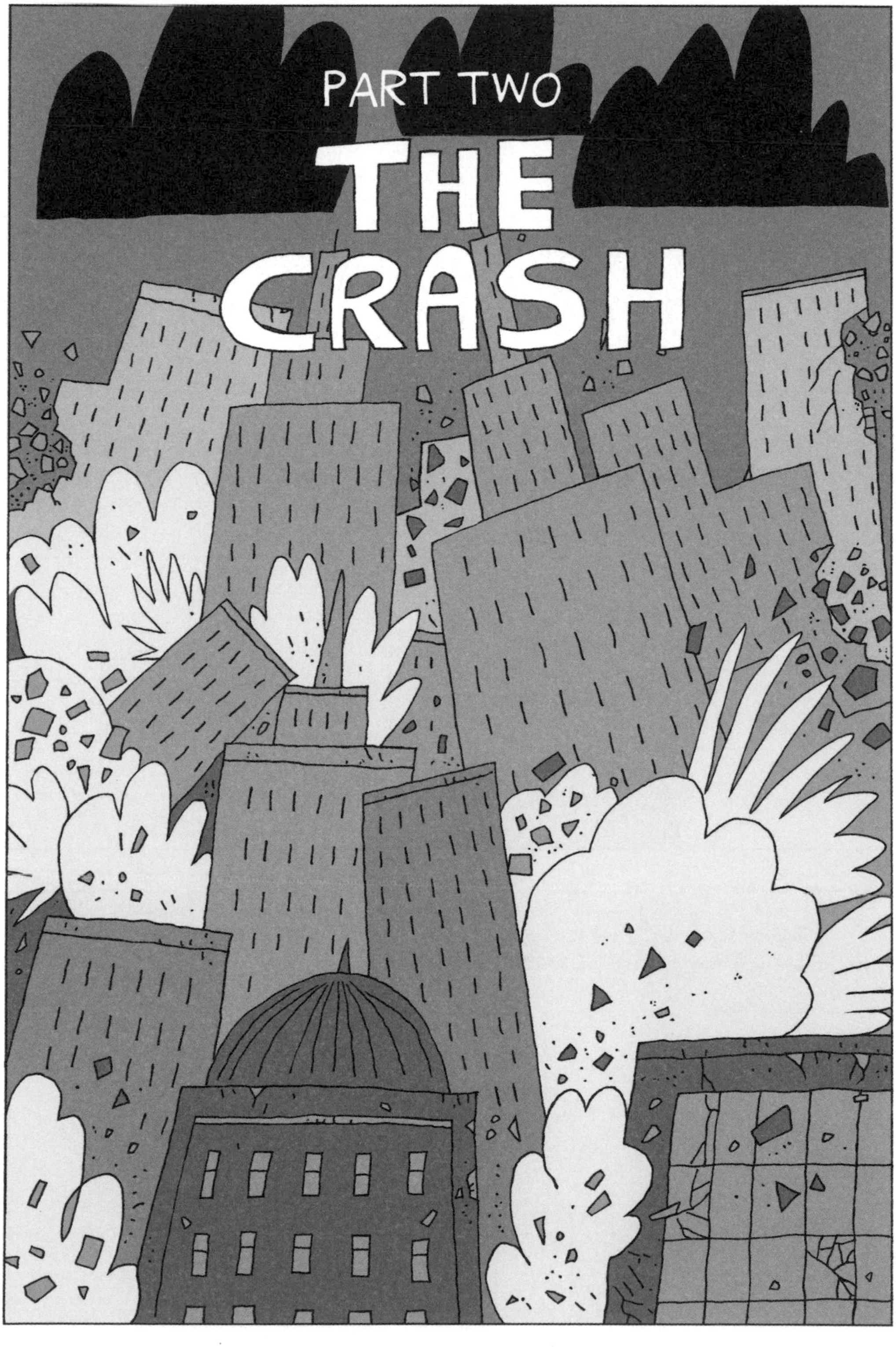
PART TWO
THE CRASH

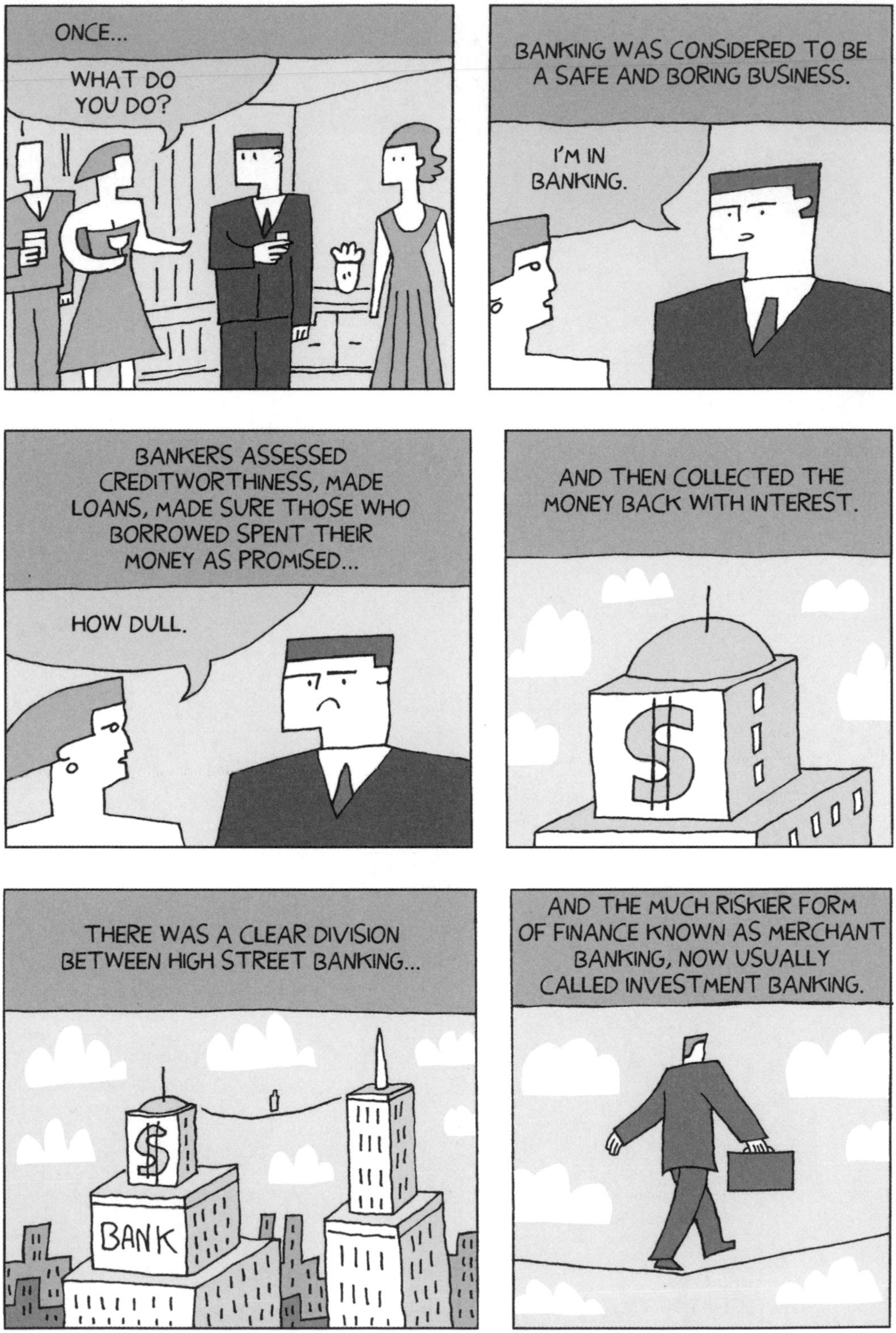
ONCE...
WHAT DO YOU DO?
BANKING WAS CONSIDERED TO BE A SAFE AND BORING BUSINESS.
I'M IN BANKING.
BANKERS ASSESSED CREDITWORTHINESS, MADE LOANS, MADE SURE THOSE WHO BORROWED SPENT THEIR MONEY AS PROMISED...
HOW DULL.
AND THEN COLLECTED THE MONEY BACK WITH INTEREST.
THERE WAS A CLEAR DIVISION BETWEEN HIGH STREET BANKING...
BANK
AND THE MUCH RISKIER FORM OF FINANCE KNOWN AS MERCHANT BANKING, NOW USUALLY CALLED INVESTMENT BANKING.

AFTER THE WALL STREET CRASH AND THE GREAT DEPRESSION, THE UNITED STATES HAD GOOD REASON TO WANT TO SAFEGUARD THIS DIVIDE. THEY PASSED THE GLASS-STEAGALL ACT (1933) THAT FORBADE HIGH STREET BANKS FROM TAKING PART IN INVESTMENT BANKING. THIS, AND OTHER ACTS OF LAW, ENSURED THAT COMMERCIAL BANKING, INVESTMENT BANKING, RESIDENTIAL MORTGAGE-LENDING, AND INSURANCE WERE DISTINCT AND TIGHTLY REGULATED INDUSTRIES.

NO ONE WANTED BANKS TAKING A CUSTOMER'S MONEY AND GAMBLING WITH IT.

WELL, ALMOST NO ONE.

AS A LIBERTARIAN, I FIND THIS TO BE AN UNACCEPTABLE CONSTRAINT BY THE GOVERNMENT ON THE FREE MARKET.

SO WHAT IS AN INVESTMENT BANK, COMPARED TO A HIGH STREET BANK?

AN INVESTMENT BANK HELPS INDIVIDUALS, CORPORATIONS, AND GOVERNMENTS RAISE MONEY, BUT CAN ALSO ACT AS THEIR AGENT OR ADVISER IN FINANCIAL ISSUES.

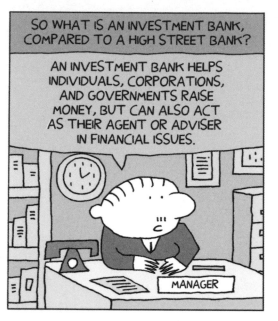

FOR EXAMPLE, A BIG CORPORATION MIGHT ASK FOR A BANK'S HELP IF IT WANTS TO BORROW MONEY IN THE BOND MARKETS, OR FLOAT ITSELF ON THE STOCK MARKET, OR BUY UP ANOTHER COMPANY.

BUT AN INVESTMENT BANK ALSO DOES SOMETHING QUITE DIFFERENT— IT DEALS DIRECTLY IN FINANCIAL MARKETS ON ITS OWN ACCOUNT. IT MAKES MONEY BY BUYING FINANCIAL ASSETS FROM ONE CLIENT AND SELLING THEM TO ANOTHER — OFTEN WITH A HEFTY MARK-UP.

HIGH STREET OR RETAIL BANKS, ON THE OTHER HAND, ARE BANKS THAT CONDUCT BUSINESS DIRECTLY WITH CONSUMERS. THEY OFFER SERVICES SUCH AS SAVINGS AND TRANSACTIONAL ACCOUNTS, MORTGAGES, PERSONAL LOANS, DEBIT CARDS, AND CREDIT CARDS.

IN THE OLD DAYS, INVESTMENT BANKS WERE PRIVATE PARTNERSHIPS, WHICH MEANT THAT THE CAPITAL THEY USED WAS THEIR OWN.

IF THE PARTNERS UNDERWROTE THE SALE OF A NEW ISSUE OF STOCK, THEY WERE RISKING THEIR OWN PERSONAL MONEY.

FINANCE WAS GENERALLY A STABLE BUSINESS THAT ALLOWED FOR PLENTY OF TIME ON THE GOLF COURSE. IT WASN'T MEANT TO BE A THRILLING ACTIVITY LIKE BASE JUMPING OR SKYDIVING.

I THINK IT'S GONE IN THE ROUGH.

BUT THINGS CHANGE.

LET'S GET BACK TO THE BANK.

IN 1981 RONALD REAGAN BECAME THE 40TH PRESIDENT OF THE UNITED STATES.

MAN IS NOT FREE UNLESS GOVERNMENT IS LIMITED.

IN AUGUST 1987, REAGAN APPOINTED ALAN GREENSPAN AS CHAIRMAN OF THE FEDERAL RESERVE.

GREENSPAN WOULD SERVE FIVE TERMS, STRETCHING ACROSS THREE DECADES AND FOUR PRESIDENCIES, WIELDING TREMENDOUS POWER AND INFLUENCE OVER US POLICY.

HELLO, LTTLE GUY!

THE POLITICAL CLIMATE HAD TURNED AGAINST BIG GOVERNMENT AND TOWARDS DEREGULATION. GREENSPAN INTENDED TO TAKE FULL ADVANTAGE OF THIS.

I'M GOING TO CUT YOU DOWN TO SIZE.

IT DIDN'T QUITE WORK OUT THAT WAY. REAGAN EXPANDED GOVERNMENT BY MASSIVELY INCREASING MILITARY SPENDING.

YIKES!

WHERE THERE WAS FREE MARKET SUCCESS WAS IN THE GRADUAL EROSION OF BANKING REGULATIONS.

IN 1996, THE FEDERAL RESERVE ALLOWED BANK HOLDING COMPANIES TO OWN INVESTMENT BANKING OPERATIONS THAT ACCOUNTED FOR 25 PER CENT OF THEIR REVENUES.

GREENSPAN! WE NEED YOU TO BREAK DOWN THAT WALL SO WE CAN ACCESS THAT HUGE PILE OF MONEY.

THIS DECISION EFFECTIVELY MADE GLASS-STEAGALL OBSOLETE, AS VIRTUALLY ANY BANK WOULD BE ABLE TO STAY WITHIN THESE LIMITS.

THANKS, BUDDY!

IN 1998, TRAVELERS INSURANCE GROUP AND CITICORP ANNOUNCED THEIR PLANS TO MERGE.

LET'S GET MARRIED.

YAY!

THE DEAL WAS TECHNICALLY ILLEGAL, SO BEFORE THE MERGER WENT AHEAD...

RING!

EXECUTIVES PLACED PERSONAL CALLS TO ALAN GREENSPAN...

HELLO!

TREASURY SECRETARY ROBERT RUBIN...

YES!

AND PRESIDENT BILL CLINTON.

HEY THERE!

AS THE LAW STOOD, THE BANK WOULD HAVE TWO YEARS TO DIVEST ITSELF OF ITS INSURANCE BUSINESS.

HEE HEE!

HOWEVER, BANK EXECUTIVES WERE CONFIDENT THAT GLASS-STEAGALL WOULD BE REPEALED BEFORE THEN.

DON'T WORRY.

IN THINKING THIS, THEY WERE QUITE CORRECT. THE 1999 GRAMM-LEACH-BLILEY ACT DELIVERED THE FINAL DEATH BLOW TO GLASS-STEAGALL.

THEY'RE JOKINGLY CALLING IT THE CITIGROUP RELIEF ACT. HA!

CITIGROUP BECAME THE WORLD'S LARGEST FINANCIAL SERVICES COMPANY, FORMED BY WHAT WAS, AT THAT TIME, THE BIGGEST CORPORATE MERGER EVER.

SOON AFTERWARDS, ROBERT RUBIN RESIGNED FROM THE TREASURY TO BECOME VICE-CHAIRMAN AND EVENTUALLY CHAIRMAN OF CITIGROUP.

BE MINE.

OVER THE NEXT DECADE HE MADE OVER 120 MILLION DOLLARS.

THROUGHOUT THE CLINTON ERA, THE FINANCIAL SECTOR'S MAJOR COMPONENTS – BROKERAGE, SECURITIES TRADING, INSURANCE, AND DERIVATIVES – WERE ALL CONSOLIDATED INTO A SMALL GROUP OF GIGANTIC FIRMS THAT OFTEN CO-OPERATED WITH EACH OTHER, PARTICULARLY IN LOBBYING AND POLITICS.

THE DOWNSIDE OF THESE CHANGES WAS THAT THEY MADE THE SYSTEM FRAGILE, INTERDEPENDENT, AND VULNERABLE TO FRAUD AND CRISIS. SOMETHING KNOWN AS SYSTEMIC RISK.

BUT WHAT REALLY BROUGHT THE PARTY TO AN END WAS DERIVATIVES.

DERIVATIVES HAVE BEEN A LONG-STANDING FEATURE OF FINANCIAL MARKETS.

IMAGINE A FARMER WHO WANTS TO SET A PRICE FOR CATTLE HE'LL NOT SELL FOR ANOTHER YEAR.

I'M WORRIED THAT THE PRICE WILL FALL BETWEEN THEN AND NOW AND I'LL LOSE OUT.

IN COMES A BROKER, WORKING ON BEHALF OF AN INVESTOR.

HEY!

MY INVESTOR BELIEVES THAT CATTLE PRICES ARE GOING TO SHOOT UP IN THE COMING YEAR, SO HE'LL GLADLY BUY FROM YOU AT THE CURRENT VALUE.

EACH SIDE OF THE DEAL IS MAKING A BET ON THE MARKET PRICE OF A COMMODITY IN THE FUTURE. WHICH IS WHY SUCH A DERIVATIVE IS CALLED A FUTURE.

IF CATTLE PRICES DO RISE OVER THE COMING YEAR, THEN MY INVESTOR WILL MAKE A TIDY PROFIT WHEN THE HERD IS SOLD.

AND, IF THE PRICE FALLS, THEN I'LL SELL THE DERIVATIVE ON TO SOMEONE ELSE BEFORE MY INVESTOR MAKES A HEAVY LOSS.

AND THIS IS THE MAIN THING TO UNDERSTAND HERE – DERIVATIVES CAN BE TRADED IN THEIR OWN RIGHT. THE NAME COMES FROM THE FACT THAT THEIR VALUE DERIVES FROM THEIR UNDERLYING PRODUCT.

WALL STREET.

ANOTHER FORM OF DERIVATIVE IS AN OPTION.

LET'S SAY YOU WANT TO MAKE MONEY BY BUYING AND THEN SELLING A LUXURY CAR.

AN OPTION WILL GIVE YOU THE RIGHT, BUT NOT THE OBLIGATION, TO BUY THE CAR AT A SPECIFIED FUTURE DATE, FOR A SPECIFIED PRICE. SO YOU SPEND $500 ON AN OPTION THAT WILL ALLOW YOU TO BUY THE CAR FOR $50,000 IN A YEAR'S TIME.

THE YEAR PASSES AND THE CAR IS ON SALE FOR $60,000.

BY THEN RESELLING THE CAR, YOU'LL HAVE A PROFIT OF $10,000, MINUS THE $500 YOU SPENT ON THE OPTION.

IF THE PRICE OF THE CAR FALLS, THEN THE OPTION GIVES YOU THE RIGHT TO SIMPLY WALK AWAY FROM THE DEAL.

AND ALL YOU'VE LOST IS THE $500 OPTION PRICE.

NO, THANKS!

MORE EXOTIC FORMS OF DERIVATIVES EXIST. IN 1994, A TEAM OF YOUNG TRADERS FROM THE BANK J.P. MORGAN GATHERED FOR AN OFF-SITE MEETING IN BOCA RATON, FLORIDA.

MUCH DRINKING TOOK PLACE DURING THAT WEEKEND.

A JET SKI WAS TRASHED AND A SENIOR EXECUTIVE'S NOSE WAS BROKEN.

HA!

AFTER THE PARTYING WAS DONE, THE TEAM CAME UP WITH A NEW IDEA.

I'VE KNOWN PEOPLE WHO WORKED ON THE MANHATTAN PROJECT. FOR THOSE OF US ON THAT TRIP, THERE WAS THE SAME KIND OF FEELING OF BEING PRESENT AT THE CREATION OF SOMETHING INCREDIBLY IMPORTANT.

MARK C. BRICKELL

WHAT THEY CREATED WAS THE CREDIT DEFAULT SWAP – AN INNOCUOUS-SOUNDING DERIVATIVE...

THAT YEARS LATER...

WOULD CONTRIBUTE TO A WORLDWIDE FINANCIAL CATASTROPHE.

SO WHAT IS A CDS?

HERE'S MARY, WHO WANTS TO BORROW MONEY TO RENOVATE HER HOUSE.

HI!

JIM OFFERS TO LEND HER THE MONEY.

HELLO!

JIM ISN'T DOING THIS OUT OF THE KINDNESS OF HIS OWN HEART. MARY HAS AGREED TO PAY HIM A GOOD RATE OF INTEREST.

I HAVE MONEY COMING IN EVERY MONTH.

AFTER A FEW MONTHS, JIM BEGINS TO WORRY THAT MARY WON'T BE ABLE TO PAY OFF THE LOAN.

HOWEVER, AT THIS POINT, HE HAS A BRILLIANT IDEA.

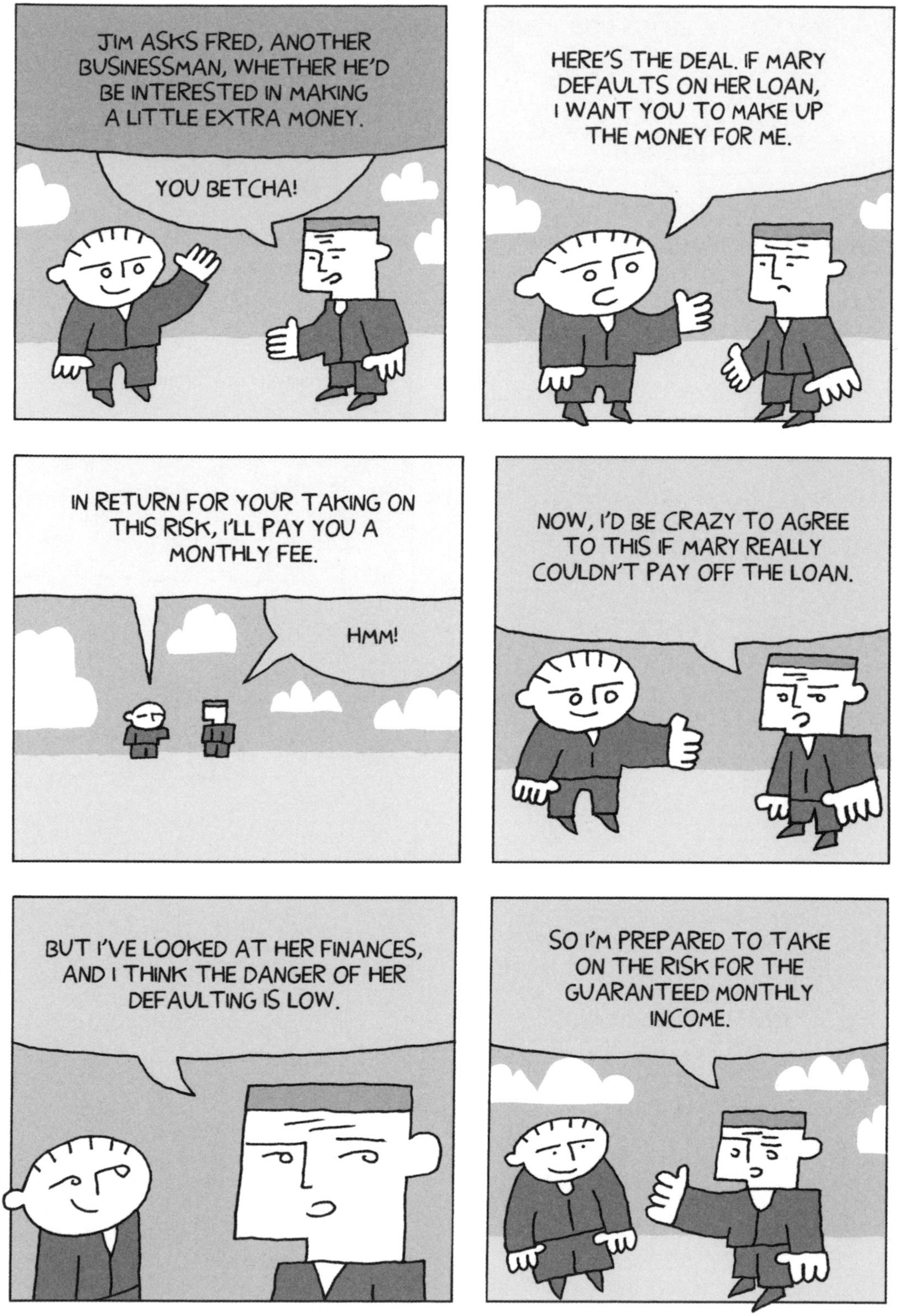
JIM ASKS FRED, ANOTHER BUSINESSMAN, WHETHER HE'D BE INTERESTED IN MAKING A LITTLE EXTRA MONEY.
YOU BETCHA!
HERE'S THE DEAL. IF MARY DEFAULTS ON HER LOAN, I WANT YOU TO MAKE UP THE MONEY FOR ME.
IN RETURN FOR YOUR TAKING ON THIS RISK, I'LL PAY YOU A MONTHLY FEE.
HMM!
NOW, I'D BE CRAZY TO AGREE TO THIS IF MARY REALLY COULDN'T PAY OFF THE LOAN.
BUT I'VE LOOKED AT HER FINANCES, AND I THINK THE DANGER OF HER DEFAULTING IS LOW.
SO I'M PREPARED TO TAKE ON THE RISK FOR THE GUARANTEED MONTHLY INCOME.

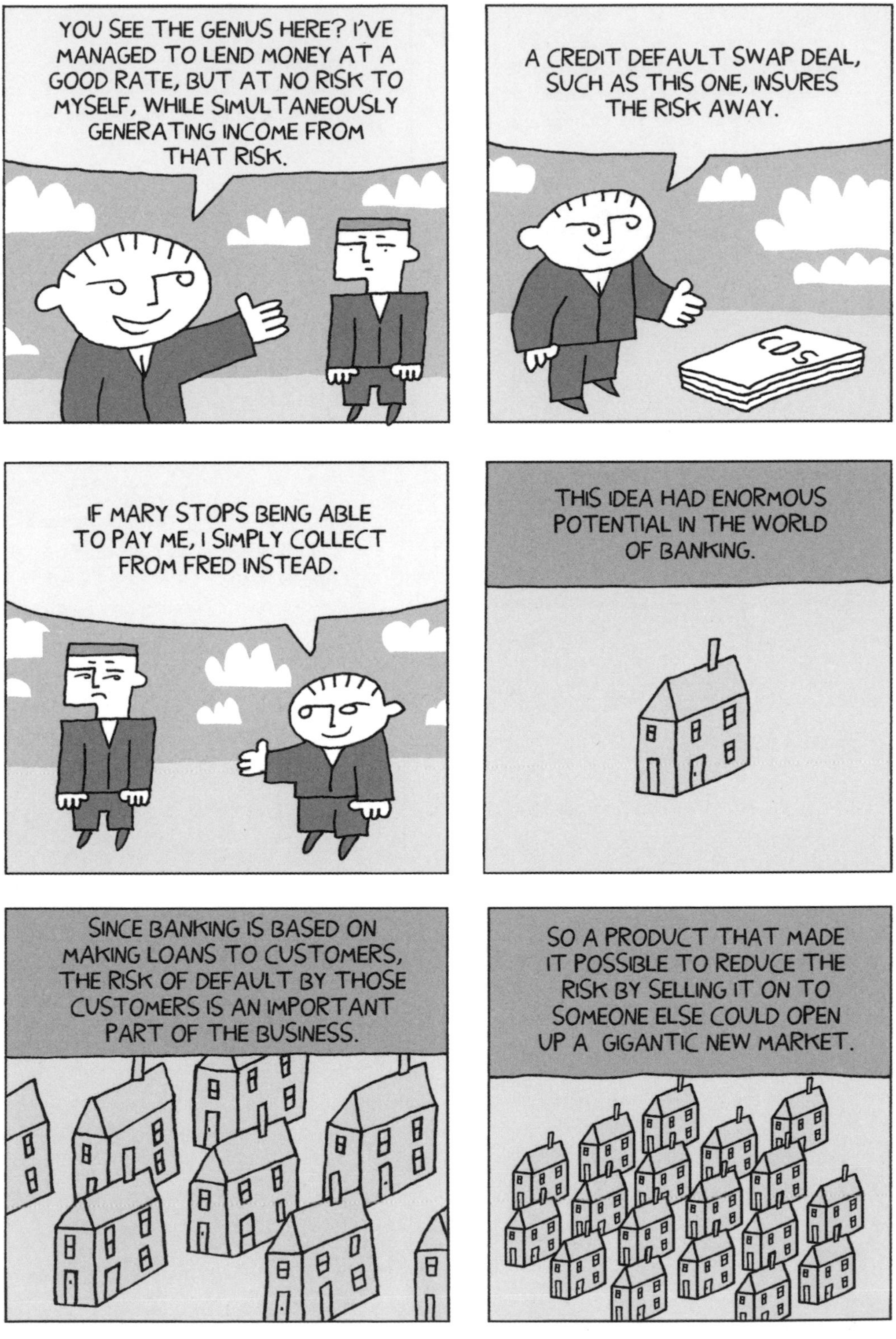
YOU SEE THE GENIUS HERE? I'VE MANAGED TO LEND MONEY AT A GOOD RATE, BUT AT NO RISK TO MYSELF, WHILE SIMULTANEOUSLY GENERATING INCOME FROM THAT RISK.
A CREDIT DEFAULT SWAP DEAL, SUCH AS THIS ONE, INSURES THE RISK AWAY.
CDS
IF MARY STOPS BEING ABLE TO PAY ME, I SIMPLY COLLECT FROM FRED INSTEAD.
THIS IDEA HAD ENORMOUS POTENTIAL IN THE WORLD OF BANKING.
SINCE BANKING IS BASED ON MAKING LOANS TO CUSTOMERS, THE RISK OF DEFAULT BY THOSE CUSTOMERS IS AN IMPORTANT PART OF THE BUSINESS.
SO A PRODUCT THAT MADE IT POSSIBLE TO REDUCE THE RISK BY SELLING IT ON TO SOMEONE ELSE COULD OPEN UP A GIGANTIC NEW MARKET.

THERE IS A FURTHER COMPLICATION TO WHAT A CDS IS.

NORMALLY, WHEN YOU INSURE SOMETHING, LIKE YOUR HOUSE, YOU HAVE TO OWN IT. IF IT BURNS DOWN THE INSURANCE COMPANY PAYS UP.

BUT WITH A CDS IT ISN'T NECESSARY TO OWN WHAT YOU ARE INSURING.

I THINK I'LL MAKE A BET ON THOSE THREE HOUSES OVER THERE.

IMAGINE IF EVERYONE IN YOUR STREET, OR YOUR TOWN, INSURED YOUR HOUSE TOO.

IF IT BURNS DOWN, THE INSURER HAS TO PAY OUT, NOT ONCE, BUT MANY TIMES.

SPECULATORS GOBBLED UP CDSs JUST TO GAMBLE ON FAILURE. RISK WAS NO LONGER BEING LESSENED, BUT MAGNIFIED.

YIKES!

CDS

THERE WAS NO UPPER LIMIT TO HOW MUCH LOSS COULD BE CREATED BY ONE SINGLE DEFAULT OR FAILURE.

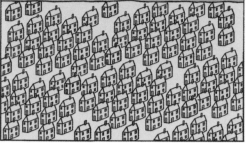

BY MARCH 1998, THE GLOBAL CDS MARKET WAS ESTIMATED AT ABOUT $300 BILLION. FOUR YEARS LATER, BY THE END OF 2002, THE OUTSTANDING AMOUNT WAS $2 TRILLION.

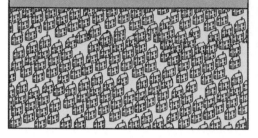

BY 2007, THE FIGURE WAS $62.2 TRILLION.

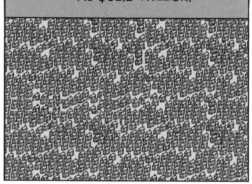

TO PUT THAT IN PERSPECTIVE, THE GROSS DOMESTIC PRODUCT OF THE US THAT YEAR WAS A MERE $13.84 TRILLION.

HOW MUCH?

A CDS CAN BE USED TO INSURE ANY LOAN, SUCH AS CAR LOANS, STUDENT LOANS, CREDIT CARD DEBT, OR BONDS.

WHAT ARE BONDS?

A BOND IS BASICALLY AN IOU. LET'S SAY A GOVERNMENT WANTS TO RAISE MONEY. TO DO THIS IT WILL ISSUE BONDS.

INVESTORS BUY THE BONDS.

HERE'S THE MONEY.

THANKS! HERE'S THE BOND.

NOW, FOR THIS MONEY, I'LL PAY YOU REGULAR INTEREST.

THAT'S GOOD.

THE BOND HAS A LIMITED LIFE. LET'S SAY TWELVE YEARS IN THIS EXAMPLE.

AT THE END OF THAT TIME, YOU'LL GET THE MONEY YOU SPENT ON THE BOND BACK, AS THE BOND WILL HAVE 'MATURED' OR COME DUE. GOVERNMENT BONDS ARE KNOWN AS GILTS IN THE UK.

THERE ARE OTHER KINDS OF BONDS APART FROM THOSE ISSUED BY GOVERNMENTS. CORPORATE BONDS ARE ISSUED BY CORPORATIONS BECAUSE THEY NEED MONEY TO EXPAND THEIR BUSINESS.

MUNICIPAL BONDS ARE ISSUED BY CITIES OR STATES TO RAISE MONEY TO BUILD ROADS OR FUND OTHER INFRASTRUCTURE PROJECTS.

I SEE!

THE GROWTH OF THE CDS MARKET USEFULLY SPREAD RISK, BUT IT ALSO DANGEROUSLY INTER-LINKED THE WHOLE FINANCIAL SYSTEM.

IT WAS LIKE A HUGE PILE OF DRY TIMBER, JUST WAITING FOR A SPARK.

THAT SPARK CAME FROM THE US HOUSING MARKET.

IN 2002, ALAN GREENSPAN, IN AN ATTEMPT TO STIMULATE THE ECONOMY, SET INTEREST RATES AT ONE PER CENT – THE LOWEST FOR FIFTY YEARS.

THE LOW INTEREST RATE MEANT THAT IT WAS EASY FOR BUSINESSES TO RAISE MONEY CHEAPLY AND ALSO FOR CONSUMERS TO BORROW OR TAKE OUT MORTGAGES.

BUT THIS LOW INTEREST RATE WAS BAD NEWS FOR INVESTORS AROUND THE WORLD.

AT A FEEBLE ONE PER CENT, THEY KNEW THAT THEY WEREN'T GOING TO MAKE MONEY FROM US TREASURY BONDS FOR SOME TIME.

THE BOOMING US HOUSING MARKET, FUELLED BY THE LOW INTEREST RATE AND WORTH TRILLIONS, BEGAN TO LOOK VERY APPEALING.

WHO WERE THESE INVESTORS?

PENSION FUNDS, INSURANCE COMPANIES, MUTUAL FUNDS, HEDGE FUNDS, FOREIGN BANKS, AND MANY OTHERS.

A HUGE DEMAND FOR REVENUES FROM MORTGAGES BEGAN, THAT WALL STREET WAS MORE THAN HAPPY TO SUPPLY.

MAKE ME MONEY.

YOU BETCHA!

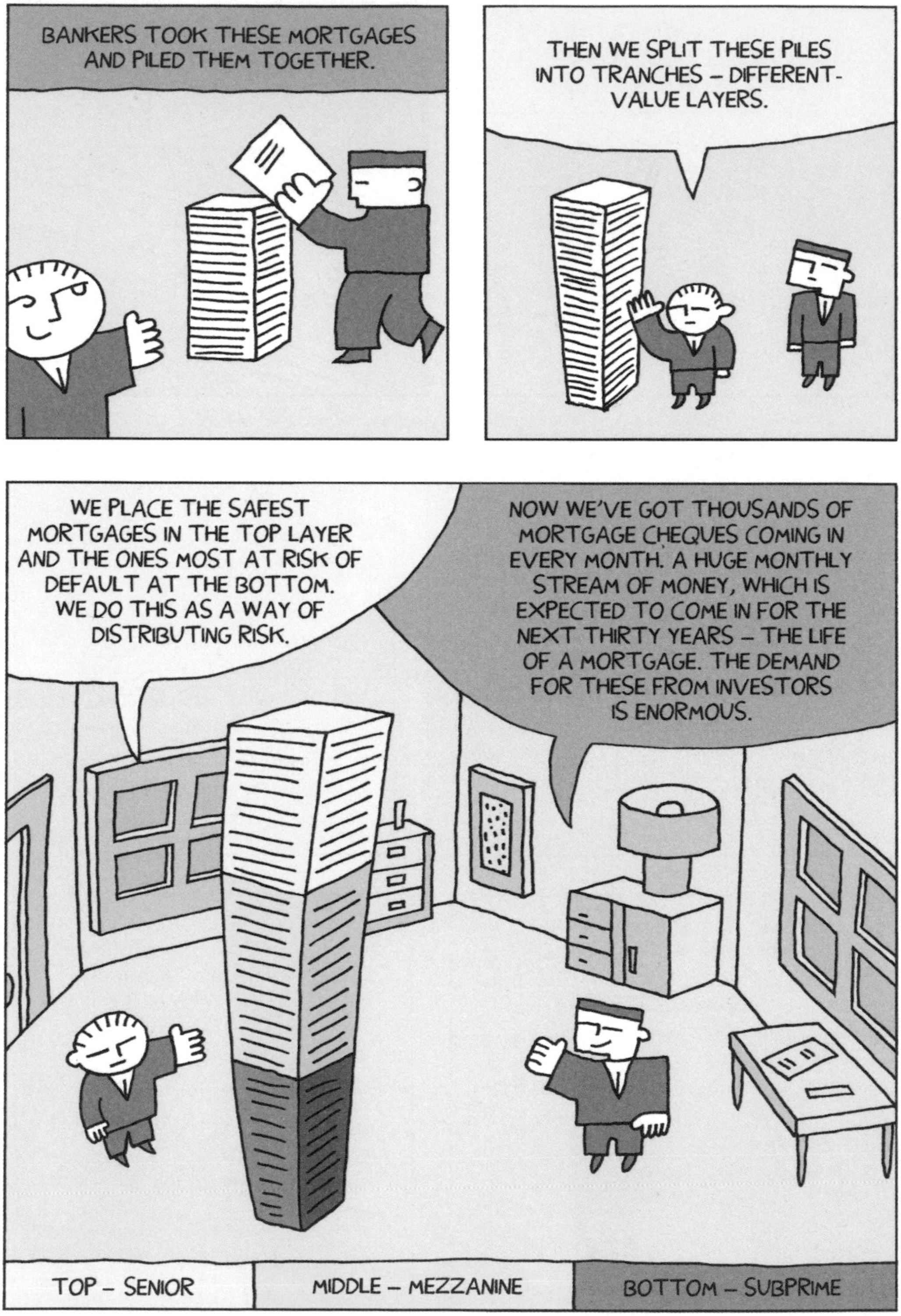
BANKERS TOOK THESE MORTGAGES AND PILED THEM TOGETHER.
THEN WE SPLIT THESE PILES INTO TRANCHES – DIFFERENT-VALUE LAYERS.
WE PLACE THE SAFEST MORTGAGES IN THE TOP LAYER AND THE ONES MOST AT RISK OF DEFAULT AT THE BOTTOM. WE DO THIS AS A WAY OF DISTRIBUTING RISK.
NOW WE'VE GOT THOUSANDS OF MORTGAGE CHEQUES COMING IN EVERY MONTH. A HUGE MONTHLY STREAM OF MONEY, WHICH IS EXPECTED TO COME IN FOR THE NEXT THIRTY YEARS – THE LIFE OF A MORTGAGE. THE DEMAND FOR THESE FROM INVESTORS IS ENORMOUS.
TOP – SENIOR
MIDDLE – MEZZANINE
BOTTOM – SUBPRIME

WHAT WE'RE DOING HERE IS CONVERTING THESE INDIVIDUAL LOANS INTO MARKETABLE SECURITIES, SO THAT WE CAN SELL THEM ON TO INVESTORS.

IT'S THE STUFF DOWN HERE THAT YOU HAVE TO KEEP AN EYE ON. 'SUBPRIME' MEANS THAT IT'S AT RISK OF DEFAULT

IT SHOULDN'T MATTER, THOUGH, BECAUSE THE SUPER-SAFE SENIOR RATE SHOULD BALANCE OUT ANY DANGERS. THIS WHOLE BUNDLE HAS A NAME. IT'S A CALLED A COLLATERALISED DEBT OBLIGATION.

WHAT MAKES IT EVEN SAFER IS THAT LOANS ARE BUNDLED FROM DIFFERENT PARTS OF THE COUNTRY, SO THE CHANCE THAT THEY WILL ALL GO BAD AT THE SAME TIME IS REMOTE.

BANKS WORKED OUT A WAY OF KEEPING CDOs OFF THEIR BOOKS, BY MOVING THEM TO A SHELL COMPANY CREATED FOR THIS VERY PURPOSE.

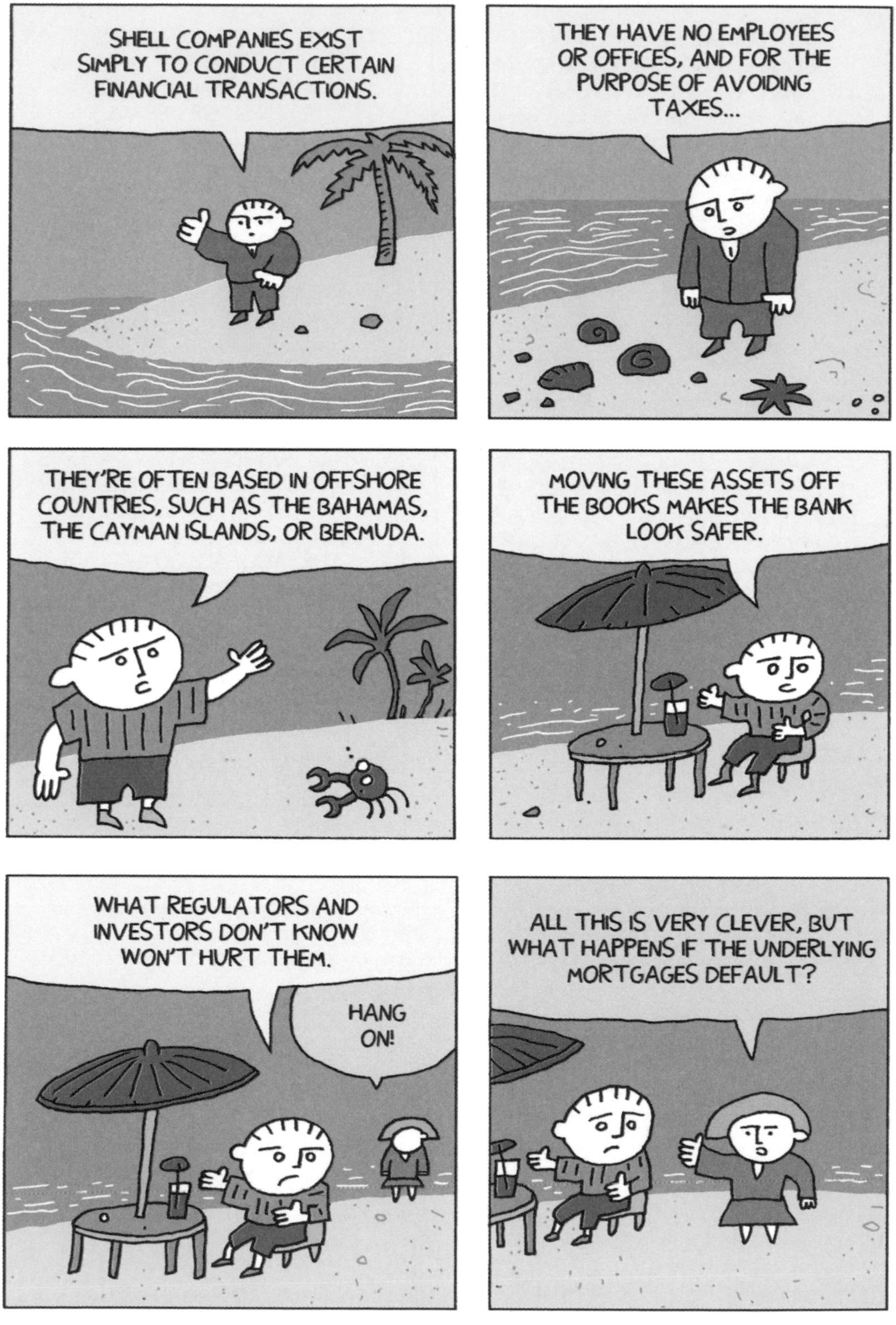
SHELL COMPANIES EXIST SIMPLY TO CONDUCT CERTAIN FINANCIAL TRANSACTIONS.
THEY HAVE NO EMPLOYEES OR OFFICES, AND FOR THE PURPOSE OF AVOIDING TAXES...
THEY'RE OFTEN BASED IN OFFSHORE COUNTRIES, SUCH AS THE BAHAMAS, THE CAYMAN ISLANDS, OR BERMUDA.
MOVING THESE ASSETS OFF THE BOOKS MAKES THE BANK LOOK SAFER.
WHAT REGULATORS AND INVESTORS DON'T KNOW WON'T HURT THEM.
HANG ON!
ALL THIS IS VERY CLEVER, BUT WHAT HAPPENS IF THE UNDERLYING MORTGAGES DEFAULT?

THIS IS WHERE THE 'GREATER FOOL' THEORY COMES INTO PLAY.

THE THEORY IS THAT THERE IS ALWAYS A GREATER FOOL, SOMEWHERE, WHO CAN BE SOLD A TOXIC LOAN AND THE DANGEROUS PIECE OF PAPER ATTACHED TO IT.

GLOBALISATION HAD OPENED UP A WHOLE WORLD OF FOOLS WHO DID NOT UNDERSTAND THE AMERICAN MORTGAGE MARKET.

NOBODY EVER THINKS THAT THEY THEMSELVES MIGHT BE THE GREATER FOOL...

CAUGHT HOLDING THE PACKAGE...

WHEN THE MUSIC STOPS.

ANY ATTEMPTS TO REGULATE THE BOOMING DERIVATIVES MARKET WERE THWARTED.

BROOKSLEY BORN, CHAIRPERSON OF THE COMMODITY FUTURES TRADING COMMISSION (CFTC) DURING THE CLINTON YEARS, SAW THE DANGERS AHEAD.

SHE MADE PUBLIC COMMENTS ABOUT THE POTENTIAL INSTABILITIES IN THE DERIVATIVES MARKET AND BEGAN A REVIEW PROCESS.

THIS TRIGGERED A FEROCIOUS RESPONSE FROM TREASURY SECRETARY ROBERT RUBIN, HIS DEPUTY LARRY SUMMERS, AND FEDERAL RESERVE CHAIRMAN ALAN GREENSPAN.

THIS WAS MORE THAN JUST A CLASSIC WASHINGTON TURF WAR - IT WAS A CLASH OF IDEOLOGIES.

GREENSPAN AND HIS ALLIES BELIEVED STRONGLY IN THE NEOLIBERAL POLICIES THAT HAD BEEN IN PLACE SINCE REAGAN.

THEIR OPPONENT, BROOKSLEY BORN, WAS NO FOOL. SHE'D BEEN PRACTISING DERIVATIVES LAW FOR TWENTY YEARS.

BORN HAD BEEN ONE OF ONLY SEVEN WOMEN IN HER CLASS AT STANFORD LAW SCHOOL.

THIS WAS IN THE EARLY 1960s AND THE VIETNAM WAR WAS RAGING.

AS A WOMAN, SHE WOULD OFTEN HEAR THIS COMMENT...

YOU'RE TAKING THE PLACE OF A MAN WHO COULD BE HERE AND NOT HAVE TO GO TO WAR.

SHE GRADUATED TOP OF HER CLASS AND WAS THE FIRST FEMALE PRESIDENT OF THE STANFORD LAW REVIEW.

ON GAINING THIS HONOUR, SHE RECEIVED A PHONE CALL FROM ONE OF THE SCHOOL'S DEANS.

DRING!

BROOKSLEY! I JUST WANT YOU TO KNOW THAT THE FACULTY STANDS READY TO STEP IN IF YOU'RE NOT ABLE TO PULL THIS OFF.

SIGH!

THE TACTIC USED BY GREENSPAN, RUBIN, AND SUMMERS TO STOP ANY ATTEMPT AT REGULATION WAS FEAR.

IF DERIVATIVES WERE REGULATED, CAPITALISM WOULD FALL APART, THEY WARNED. THERE WOULD BE MARKET TURMOIL AND RISK COULDN'T BE MANAGED EFFICIENTLY.

THEY MADE THE CLAIM THAT, BY EVEN TALKING ABOUT REGULATION, BORN WAS THREATENING THE STABILITY OF THE MARKET.

DRING!

LARRY SUMMERS TELEPHONED BORN, TELLING HER THAT HE HAD THIRTEEN ANGRY BANKERS IN HIS OFFICE WHO WERE DEMANDING SHE STOP.

THE PHONE CALL MAY HAVE BEEN ILLEGAL, AS THE CFTC IS AN INDEPENDENT BODY.

SIGH!

THE FINANCIAL MARKET LOBBIED HARD FOR LEGISLATION TO MAKE SURE THAT DERIVATIVES REMAINED UNREGULATED.

WHAT THEY GOT WAS THE COMMODITY FUTURES MODERNIZATION ACT (2000). THIS LEGISLATION WAS PASSED WITHOUT DEBATE OR REVIEW. IN EFFECT, IT BANNED REGULATORS FROM LOOKING AT DERIVATIVES. THE ARGUMENT BEING THAT THE MAIN TRADERS IN DERIVATIVES WERE BANKS AND INSTITUTIONS WHO WERE CAPABLE OF MAKING THEIR OWN ASSESSMENT OF RISK.

YIPPEE!

BROOKSLEY BORN RESIGNED.

THAT'S IT. I'M DONE.

THIS WAS WHEN THE REAL BOOM BEGAN. DERIVATIVES TRADING EXPANDED FROM $106 TRILLION IN 2001 TO A VALUE OF $531 TRILLION IN 2008.

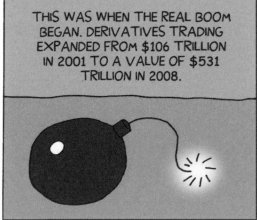

IN GREENSPAN'S MEMOIRS, 'THE AGE OF TURBULENCE', PUBLISHED IN 2007, HE BARELY MENTIONS AYN RAND OR THE THIRTY-YEAR INFLUENCE SHE HAD ON HIS LIFE.

IT'S PERHAPS UNDERSTANDABLE THAT HE'D WANT TO DISTANCE HIMSELF FROM HER ONCE HE'D REACHED HIGH OFFICE, CONSIDERING THE EXTREME POSITIONS HE'D ADVANCED AS A MEMBER OF HER COLLECTIVE.

IN 1957 HE WROTE TO THE EDITOR OF THE 'NEW YORK TIMES BOOK REVIEW', PRAISING 'ATLAS SHRUGGED'.

'ATLAS SHRUGGED' IS A CELEBRATION OF LIFE AND HAPPINESS. JUSTICE IS UNRELENTING. CREATIVE INDIVIDUALS AND UNDEVIATING PURPOSE AND RATIONALITY ACHIEVE JOY. PARASITES WHO PERSISTENTLY AVOID EITHER PURPOSE OR REASON PERISH AS THEY SHOULD.

IN 1966, GREENSPAN WROTE THREE ESSAYS FOR THE RAND ANTHOLOGY, 'CAPITALISM: THE UNKNOWN IDEAL', IN WHICH HE EQUATED GOVERNMENT REGULATION WITH A BREAKDOWN OF SOCIETY'S MORALS. IN HIS VIEW THERE WAS NO NEED FOR THE SECURITIES AND EXCHANGE COMMISSION, OR THE FOOD AND DRUG ADMINISTRATION.

ALL REGULATIONS THAT PROTECT THE PUBLIC FROM UNSCRUPULOUS BUSINESSMEN, EVEN BUILDING CODES, ARE UNNECESSARY, HE ARGUED. THE POTENTIAL DAMAGE TO A REPUTATION IS ENOUGH TO KEEP A CONTRACTOR FROM BUILDING UNSAFE STRUCTURES.

GREENSPAN GOES ON TO SAY THAT IT IS A BUSINESSMAN'S GREED THAT PROTECTS THE CONSUMER. THE REPUTATION OF A COMPANY IS OFTEN ITS MAJOR ASSET. IF A BUSINESS ISN'T TRUSTED, THEN IT CANNOT PROSPER. THIS IS EVEN TRUER FOR A SECURITIES FIRM.

SECURITIES WORTH HUNDREDS OF MILLIONS OF DOLLARS ARE TRADED EVERY DAY OVER THE TELEPHONE. THE SLIGHTEST DOUBT AS TO THE TRUSTWORTHINESS OF THE BROKER'S WORD OR COMMITMENT WOULD PUT HIM OUT OF BUSINESS OVERNIGHT.

IT IS CLEAR FROM THESE ESSAYS THAT RAND PROFOUNDLY INFLUENCED GREENSPAN'S ECONOMIC THINKING. IT ALSO EXPLAINS WHY, ONCE HE BECAME CHAIRMAN OF THE FEDERAL RESERVE, HE TOOK SUCH A HANDS-OFF APPROACH TO THE REGULATION OF DERIVATIVES. A DECISION THAT WAS TO PROVE CATASTROPHIC FOR THE WORLD.

BUT ISN'T THERE A FORM OF REGULATION ANYWAY? AREN'T THERE COMPANIES WHOSE JOB IT IS TO JUDGE THE QUALITY OF DERIVATIVES?

THE BIG THREE CREDIT RATING AGENCIES ARE STANDARD AND POOR'S, MOODY'S, AND FITCH RATINGS.

I'D LIKE YOU TO RATE THIS LOT.

HMM!

THESE COMPANIES ARE HIRED BY BANKS TO EVALUATE THE WORTH OF FINANCIAL PRODUCTS, LIKE DERIVATIVES.

I THINK THIS IS A TRIPLE B.

BUT ANY FOOL CAN SEE THAT THERE IS A BASIC CONFLICT OF INTEREST HERE.

ARE YOU SURE?

THE BANKS PAID THE RATING AGENCIES A BIG FEE FOR THIS WORK.

ER...

SO THERE WAS AN INCENTIVE TO PLEASE THOSE WHO WERE PAYING THEM.

IT MUST BE A TRIPLE A.

AND COMPETITION ONLY MADE MATTERS WORSE, BECAUSE, IF ONE RATING AGENCY DIDN'T GIVE THE BANKS THE REQUIRED GRADE, THEN ANOTHER COULD BE CHOSEN.

SO MUCH FOR THE CORRECTIONAL POWER OF THE FREE MARKET.

DURING THE HOUSING BUBBLE, COLOSSAL AMOUNTS OF MONEY WERE MADE BY THE RATING AGENCIES.

ABRACA-DABRA!

IN THE FIRST WEEK OF JULY 2007, STANDARD AND POOR'S RATED 1,500 NEW CDOs, OR 300 PER DAY.

IT WAS AN ASSEMBLY LINE THAT TURNED CRUDDY, TOXIC SUBPRIME PRODUCTS INTO TRIPLE-A-RATED GOLD.

BUT WASN'T ANYONE CHECKING THE QUALITY OF THE UNDERLYING LOANS? WHAT WAS THE GOVERNMENT DOING?

GOVERNMENT PROTECTIONS DID EXIST. BACK IN 1994, BILL CLINTON HAD SIGNED INTO LAW THE HOME OWNERSHIP AND EQUITY PROTECTION ACT (HOEPA).

EZ HOME LOANS

THIS LAW WAS MEANT TO BE USED BY THE FEDERAL RESERVE BOARD TO STOP UNFAIR AND DECEPTIVE PRACTICES IN THE MORTGAGE MARKET.

I NEED A MORTGAGE.

SURE.

BUT ALAN GREENSPAN REFUSED TO USE THESE NEW POWERS.

WHERE ONCE MORE MARGINAL APPLICANTS WOULD HAVE BEEN DENIED CREDIT, LENDERS ARE NOW ABLE TO QUITE EFFECTIVELY JUDGE THE RISK POSED BY INDIVIDUAL APPLICANTS.

IT WASN'T UNTIL GREENSPAN'S SUCCESSOR, BEN BERNANKE, TOOK OVER AT THE FED THAT COMMON SENSE RULES WERE FINALLY INTRODUCED, AND EVEN THEN HE WAS TWO YEARS INTO THE JOB BEFORE HE ACTED.

LOANS LACKING DOCUMENTATION SHOWING PEOPLE CAN ACTUALLY PAY THE LOAN ARE NOW FORBIDDEN. THIS MEANS WE'RE GOING TO HAVE TO MAKE SURE PEOPLE REALLY HAVE THE MONEY.

WHAT? THAT'S CRAZY!

AND, OF COURSE, BY THEN IT WAS TOO LATE.

GREENSPAN'S NAIVE AND DANGEROUS FAITH IN COMPETITIVE MARKETS HAD ALREADY HELPED BRING ABOUT DISASTER.

THE BURNING FUSE LEADING TO THIS CATASTROPHE WAS THE MORTGAGE SECURITISATION CHAIN.

HERE, VERY SIMPLY, IS HOW THE CHAIN WORKED. HOMEOWNERS BOUGHT MORTGAGES FROM MORTGAGE PROVIDERS.

THESE PROVIDERS DIDN'T HAVE TO WORRY WHETHER HOMEOWNERS WERE AT RISK OF DEFAULT, AS THEY WOULD IMMEDIATELY SELL THE MORTGAGES TO WALL STREET.

WALL STREET WOULD THEN SECURITISE THESE LOANS, BUNDLING THEM TOGETHER AS COLLATERALISED DEBT OBLIGATIONS (CDOs), AS PREVIOUSLY DESCRIBED.

WALL STREET THEN SOLD THESE BUNDLES ON TO INVESTORS AROUND THE WORLD.

AND CREDIT DEFAULT SWAPS, WHICH WERE MEANT TO MAKE LENDING SAFER, IN THE END NOT ONLY SPREAD BUT MAGNIFIED RISK.

FROM 2003 THROUGH TO MID-2007, AMERICA'S FINANCIAL SECTOR CHURNED OUT THREE TRILLION DOLLARS OF OFTEN FRAUDULENT MORTGAGE-BASED SECURITIES. THE HOME LOANS UNDERLYING THESE SECURITIES WERE MOSTLY SOURCED THROUGH A NEW BREED OF UNREGULATED MORTGAGE BANKS.

MORE THAN HALF THE INCREASE IN LENDING DURING THE BUBBLE WAS ACCOUNTED FOR BY SUBPRIME LOANS AT HIGH RISK OF DEFAULT.

THESE BORROWERS WERE PEOPLE WHO WERE UNDER FINANCIAL PRESSURE, PEOPLE WHO WERE SPECULATING, PEOPLE WHO WERE COMMITTING FRAUD, OR PEOPLE WHO WERE BEING DEFRAUDED OUTRIGHT.

AFTER THE CRASH, CHRISTOPHER WARREN, A LOAN OFFICER FOR AMERIQUEST, POSTED A CONFESSION ONLINE.

MY MANAGERS AND HANDLERS TAUGHT ME THE INS AND OUTS OF MORTGAGE FRAUD, DRUGS, SEX, AND MONEY, MONEY, AND MORE MONEY.

MY FRIEND AND MANAGER HANDED OUT CRYSTAL METHAMPHETAMINE TO LOAN OFFICERS IN A BID TO KEEP THEM UP AND AT WORK LONG HOURS.

AT ANY GIVEN MOMENT COCAINE AND METH WAS BEING SNORTED INSIDE THE RESTROOMS.

MORE THAN HALF THE STAFF WAS MANIPULATING DOCUMENTS TO GET LOANS TO FUND, AND MORE THAN 75 PER CENT JUST MADE COMPLETELY FALSE STATEMENTS.

A TYPICAL 'WELCOME ABOARD' GIFT WAS A PAIR OF SCISSORS, TAPE, AND WHITE OUT. THREE THINGS A FINANCIAL PROFESSIONAL SHOULD NEVER NEED.

AFTER POSTING THIS CONFESSION, WARREN TRIED TO LEAVE THE US, BUT WAS ARRESTED AT THE CANADIAN BORDER.

HE HAD ONE MILLION IN SWISS FRANC CERTIFICATES AND SEVENTY THOUSAND DOLLARS STUFFED INTO HIS COWBOY BOOTS.

AMERIQUEST CLAIMED THAT WARREN WAS NOT A TYPICAL EMPLOYEE. HOWEVER, IT IS A FACT THAT AGGRESSIVE PRACTICES WERE WIDESPREAD AT THE HEIGHT OF THE HOUSING BUBBLE.

THE ENORMOUS DEMAND FOR MORTGAGES FROM WALL STREET GENERATED FIERCE COMPETITION BETWEEN MORTGAGE SUPPLIERS, AND THIS DEMAND DROVE DOWN THE QUALITY OF THE LOANS.

IT WAS A RACE TO THE BOTTOM. WE FOUND THAT THE GUIDELINES ON WHO WE COULD LEND TO WERE GETTING LOOSER EVERY MONTH.

IN A 2005 REPORT, THE FBI NOTED THAT...

A SIGNIFICANT FRACTION OF THE MORTGAGE INDUSTRY IS DEVOID OF ANY MANDATORY FRAUD REPORTING. BASED ON VARIOUS INDUSTRY REPORTS AND FBI ANALYSIS, MORTGAGE FRAUD IS PERVASIVE AND GROWING.

EIGHTY PER CENT OF ALL REPORTED FRAUD CASES INVOLVED COLLABORATION OR COLLUSION BY INDUSTRY INSIDERS.

THIS MEANS ESTATE AGENTS, MORTGAGE BROKERS, LENDERS, OR SOME COMBINATION OF THE ABOVE.

THOSE WHO WOULD LIKE TO BLAME THE SUBPRIME MORTGAGE DISASTER ON THE POOR COMMITTING FRAUD AGAINST THE MORTGAGE INDUSTRY SHOULD TAKE A CLOSER LOOK AT THE FACTS.

THEY WHAT?

IN 2007, A WOMAN NAMED EILEEN FOSTER WAS PROMOTED TO SENIOR VICE PRESIDENT FOR FRAUD RISK MANAGEMENT AT COUNTRYWIDE FINANCIAL CORPORATION.

IT WASN'T LONG BEFORE FOSTER AND HER TEAM DISCOVERED WIDESPREAD FRAUD IN MULTIPLE REGIONAL OFFICES.

YOU GOT ANY WHITE OUT?

AS WAS COMMON PRACTICE, LOAN OFFICERS WERE BEING COMPENSATED REGARDLESS OF THE QUALITY OF THE LOANS.

SURE!

THEY HAD FINANCIAL INCENTIVES TO PRODUCE LOANS WITH THE HIGHEST POSSIBLE INTEREST RATES AND FEES.

YOU GUYS!

THE COMPANY WAS FORCED TO CLOSE SIX OF ITS EIGHT OFFICES IN THE BOSTON AREA.

YOU'RE FIRED.

IN DECEMBER 2011, FOSTER WAS INTERVIEWED ON THE US TV PROGRAMME '60 MINUTES'.

DO YOU BELIEVE THAT THERE ARE PEOPLE AT COUNTRYWIDE WHO BELONG BEHIND BARS?

YES!

DO YOU WANT TO GIVE ME THEIR NAMES?

NO.

WOULD YOU GIVE THEIR NAMES TO A GRAND JURY IF YOU WERE ASKED?

YES.

HOW MUCH FRAUD WAS THERE AT COUNTRYWIDE?

FROM WHAT I SAW, THE TYPES OF THINGS I SAW, IT WAS – IT APPEARED TO BE SYSTEMIC.

IT WASN'T JUST ONE INDIVIDUAL OR TWO OR THREE INDIVIDUALS, IT WAS BRANCHES OF INDIVIDUALS. IT WAS REGIONS OF INDIVIDUALS.

WHAT YOU SEEM TO BE SAYING IS, IT WAS A WAY OF DOING BUSINESS?

YES.

WHAT WAS GOING ON IN BOSTON WAS ALSO GOING ON IN CHICAGO, AND MIAMI, AND DETROIT, LAS VEGAS, AND, YOU KNOW, PHOENIX, AND IN ALL THE BIG MARKETS ALL OVER FLORIDA.

I CAME TO FIND OUT THAT THERE WERE MANY, MANY, MANY REPORTS OF FRAUD AS I HAD SUSPECTED, AND THOSE WERE NEVER — THEY WERE NEVER REPORTED TO THE BOARD, NEVER REPORTED TO ME, NEVER REPORTED TO THE GOVERNMENT WHILE I WAS THERE.

AND YOU BELIEVE THIS WAS INTENTIONAL?

YES.

THE CHAIRMAN AND CHIEF EXECUTIVE OF COUNTRYWIDE WAS THE FEARSOME ANGELO MOZILO.

GRR!

SON OF A BRONX BUTCHER, HE'D FOUNDED THE COMPANY IN 1969 WITH HIS MENTOR, DAVID LOEB.

ORIGINALLY MOZILO WAS VERY CONCERNED OVER THE QUALITY OF CREDIT BORROWERS AND THEIR LOANS.

WHEN SUBPRIME LOANS FIRST CAME ONTO THE SCENE IN THE LATE 1980s, HIS COMPANY DID NOT TAKE PART.

THESE NEW GUYS ARE CROOKS.

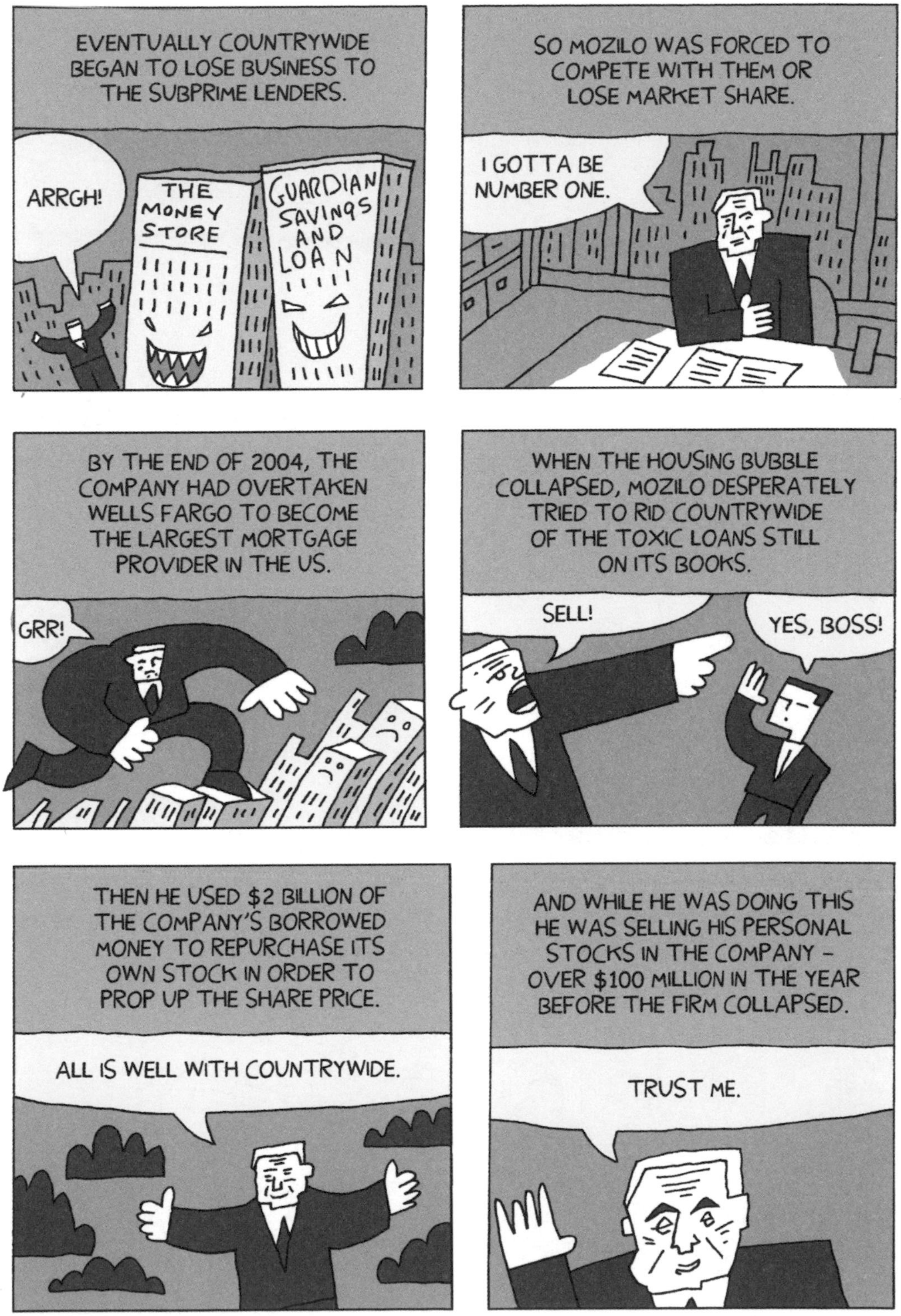
EVENTUALLY COUNTRYWIDE BEGAN TO LOSE BUSINESS TO THE SUBPRIME LENDERS.
ARRGH!
THE MONEY STORE
GUARDIAN SAVINGS AND LOAN
SO MOZILO WAS FORCED TO COMPETE WITH THEM OR LOSE MARKET SHARE.
I GOTTA BE NUMBER ONE.
BY THE END OF 2004, THE COMPANY HAD OVERTAKEN WELLS FARGO TO BECOME THE LARGEST MORTGAGE PROVIDER IN THE US.
GRR!
WHEN THE HOUSING BUBBLE COLLAPSED, MOZILO DESPERATELY TRIED TO RID COUNTRYWIDE OF THE TOXIC LOANS STILL ON ITS BOOKS.
SELL!
YES, BOSS!
THEN HE USED $2 BILLION OF THE COMPANY'S BORROWED MONEY TO REPURCHASE ITS OWN STOCK IN ORDER TO PROP UP THE SHARE PRICE.
ALL IS WELL WITH COUNTRYWIDE.
AND WHILE HE WAS DOING THIS HE WAS SELLING HIS PERSONAL STOCKS IN THE COMPANY – OVER $100 MILLION IN THE YEAR BEFORE THE FIRM COLLAPSED.
TRUST ME.

MOZILO LOOKED AROUND FOR A GREATER FOOL AND FOUND ONE IN BANK OF AMERICA, WHO BOUGHT THE COMPANY FOR $4.5 BILLION.

THE ACQUISITION OF COUNTRYWIDE WAS TO PROVE COSTLY FOR THE BUYER.

THE COMPANY CONTINUED TO LOSE BILLIONS AND BECAME THE SUBJECT OF A FEDERAL FRAUD INVESTIGATION.

IN THE END, BANK OF AMERICA HAD TO PAY OUT A $335 MILLION SETTLEMENT TO THE TREASURY DEPARTMENT.

MOZILO WAS CHARGED BY THE SECURITIES AND EXCHANGE COMMISSION WITH INSIDER TRADING.

HE AGREED TO PAY $67.5 MILLION IN FINES AND ACCEPTED A LIFETIME BAN FROM SERVING AS AN OFFICER OR DIRECTOR OF ANY PUBLIC COMPANY.

HARDLY A BIG DEAL FOR A MAN ESTIMATED TO BE WORTH $600 MILLION AND WHO WAS ON THE VERGE OF RETIREMENT ANYWAY.

I FEEL GOOD.

BY SEPTEMBER 2008, AVERAGE US HOUSING PRICES HAD FALLEN BY OVER 20 PER CENT FROM THEIR MID-2006 PEAK.

AS PRICES FELL, BORROWERS WITH VARIABLE RATE MORTGAGES AND THOSE WITH FIXED RATES COMING TO AN END COULD NOT REFINANCE TO AVOID HIGHER PAYMENTS CONNECTED WITH RISING INTEREST RATES. THEY BEGAN TO DEFAULT.

DURING 2007, LENDERS BEGAN FORECLOSURE PROCEEDINGS ON NEARLY 1.3 MILLION PROPERTIES —A 79 PER CENT INCREASE OVER 2006. THEN THINGS GOT WORSE. BY AUGUST 2009, 9.2 PER CENT OF ALL US MORTGAGES WERE EITHER DELINQUENT OR IN FORECLOSURE.

ONE YEAR LATER, THIS HAD RISEN TO 14.4 PER CENT.

ARRGH!

THE PARTY WAS OVER. THE MUSIC HAD STOPPED.

THE BILL HAD TO BE PAID AT LAST.

SIR!

IN THE US, THE NEW YORK-BASED INVESTMENT BANK BEAR STEARNS WAS THE FIRST TO GO TO THE WALL.

WHIR!

TOO MANY OF THOSE SUPPOSEDLY TRIPLE-A-RATED DERIVATIVES TURNED OUT TO BE CRUD.

AIEEEE!

FOUNDED IN 1923, AND HAVING SURVIVED THE WALL STREET CRASH, BEAR STEARNS ENDED UP BEING SOLD TO J.P. MORGAN FOR TWO DOLLARS A SHARE.

IN SEPTEMBER 2008, LEHMAN BROTHERS, THE FOURTH-LARGEST INVESTMENT BANK IN THE US, FILED FOR BANKRUPTCY.

ARRGH!

FEAR GRIPPED THE MARKETS. BANKS STOPPED LENDING TO EACH OTHER...

AND THEN TO EVERYONE ELSE IN WHAT BECAME KNOWN AS THE CREDIT CRUNCH.

I'D LIKE TO BORROW MONEY SO I CAN EXPAND MY BUSINESS.

ARE YOU JOKING?

THERE WAS A FRANTIC ROUND OF CONSOLIDATIONS IN THE GLOBAL BANKING SECTOR.

MERRILL LYNCH WAS TAKEN OVER BY BANK OF AMERICA, WHILE J.P. MORGAN BOUGHT WASHINGTON MUTUAL. IN THE UK, HALIFAX BUILDING SOCIETY AND BANK OF SCOTLAND WERE ACQUIRED BY LLOYDS.

BLIMEY! WHAT HAPPENED?

THE UK BANK NORTHERN ROCK HAD OVERREACHED ITSELF BY BORROWING HEAVILY ON THE INTERNATIONAL MONEY MARKETS. IT HAD USED THAT MONEY TO EXTEND MORTGAGES TO CUSTOMERS, AND THEN RESOLD THOSE MORTGAGES TO INVESTORS.

THE SUDDEN FALLING AWAY OF INVESTOR INTEREST LEFT NORTHERN ROCK UNABLE TO PAY ITS LOANS.

WE HAVE £26.7 IN DEPOSITS, BUT WE OWE £86.7 BILLION.

AS HAPPENED WITH OTHER FINANCIAL INSTITUTIONS, THE BANK HAD NOT PUT ASIDE SUFFICIENT CAPITAL TO GET IT THROUGH DIFFICULT TIMES.

WELL, WHY WOULD WE? MONEY SAVED IS MONEY NOT BEING PUT TO WORK MAKING MORE MONEY.

WHEN CUSTOMERS HEARD THAT NORTHERN ROCK HAD APPROACHED THE BANK OF ENGLAND FOR A LOAN...

PLEASE!

IT CAUSED THE FIRST RUN ON A BRITISH BANK IN 150 YEARS.

THE STRUGGLING BANK WAS THEN TAKEN OVER BY THE GOVERNMENT. IT WAS TO BE FOUR YEARS BEFORE IT RETURNED TO PRIVATE OWNERSHIP.

BACK IN THE US, HANK PAULSON, FORMER CHAIRMAN OF GOLDMAN SACHS, WAS NOW TREASURY SECRETARY.

HI!

PAULSON WAS ANOTHER STRONG ADVOCATE OF UNFETTERED FREE MARKETS, YET, DESPITE THIS, HE THOUGHT THAT ONLY A MASSIVE INTERVENTION BY GOVERNMENT WAS GOING TO HALT THE CRISIS.

ALONG WITH FED CHAIRMAN BEN BERNANKE, HE PLEADED WITH CONGRESS TO GIVE THE TREASURY $700 BILLION WHICH HE COULD USE TO SHORE UP THE SYSTEM.

PLEASE!

THIS RESCUE EFFORT WAS CALLED THE TROUBLED ASSET RELIEF PROGRAM (TARP). PAULSON MET THE HEADS OF THE EIGHT BIGGEST BANKS AND TOLD THEM THAT THEY WOULD ALL BE TAKING MONEY FROM THE GOVERNMENT.

TARP WOULD INJECT CASH INTO THE BANKING SYSTEM, WHILE CLEANING UP THE BANK'S BALANCE SHEETS BY BUYING UP THOSE DREADED TOXIC ASSETS.

SO, WITHOUT ANY CONGRESSIONAL OVERSIGHT OR JUDICIAL REVIEW, THE US TAXPAYER ENDED UP FOOTING THE BILL FOR THE FINANCIAL INDUSTRY'S COLOSSAL INCOMPETENCE AND MALFEASANCE.

THE UK GOVERNMENT HAD TAKEN THE SAME BAILOUT PATH, BUT HAD AT LEAST ADDED SOME CONDITIONS TO ITS BILLIONS.

ALL BANKS ACCEPTING THE MONEY HAD TO THROW OUT MANAGEMENT.

THERE WERE RESTRICTIONS ON DIVIDENDS TO SHAREHOLDERS...

WHAT?

AND SYSTEMS DESIGNED TO ENCOURAGE LENDING WERE PUT IN PLACE.

I'D LIKE TO BORROW MONEY SO I CAN EXPAND MY BUSINESS.

MAYBE.

BY CONTRAST, US BANKS CONTINUED TO PAY OUT DIVIDENDS AND BONUSES.

PAULSON'S PLAN DIDN'T EVEN WORK. IT FAILED TO EITHER RESTART LENDING OR RESTORE CONFIDENCE IN THE FINANCIAL SECTOR.

OOPS!

AS THE ROTTEN CORE OF THE BANKING SYSTEM CRUMBLED, THE GLOBAL ECONOMY BEGAN TO COLLAPSE AND DISASTER HIT GREECE, IRELAND, ICELAND, AND EVENTUALLY THE EUROPEAN UNION AS A WHOLE.

IN EACH CASE, VAST AMOUNTS OF TAXPAYERS' MONEY WERE USED TO PROTECT THE BANKS.

DEBT WAS TRANSFERRED TO THE GENERAL POPULATION. BANKS KEPT ANY GAINS.

HANK PAULSON'S OLD FIRM, GOLDMAN SACHS, IS THE KING OF US BANKS—
THE COMPANY ALL OTHERS ENVY AND IMITATE. GOLDMAN'S BEHAVIOUR DURING
THE CRISIS WAS NO MORE IMMORAL THAN ITS COMPETITORS, BUT, OWING
TO ITS SKILLED AND AGGRESSIVE TACTICS, IT WAS FAR MORE SUCCESSFUL.

A CASE IN POINT IS HOW IT
CONDUCTED BUSINESS WITH
THE INSURER AMERICAN
INTERNATIONAL GROUP (AIG).

STARTING IN 2007, GOLDMAN
BEGAN BUYING INSURANCE ON $23
BILLION OF COMPLEX MORTGAGE
SECURITIES FROM THE COMPANY.

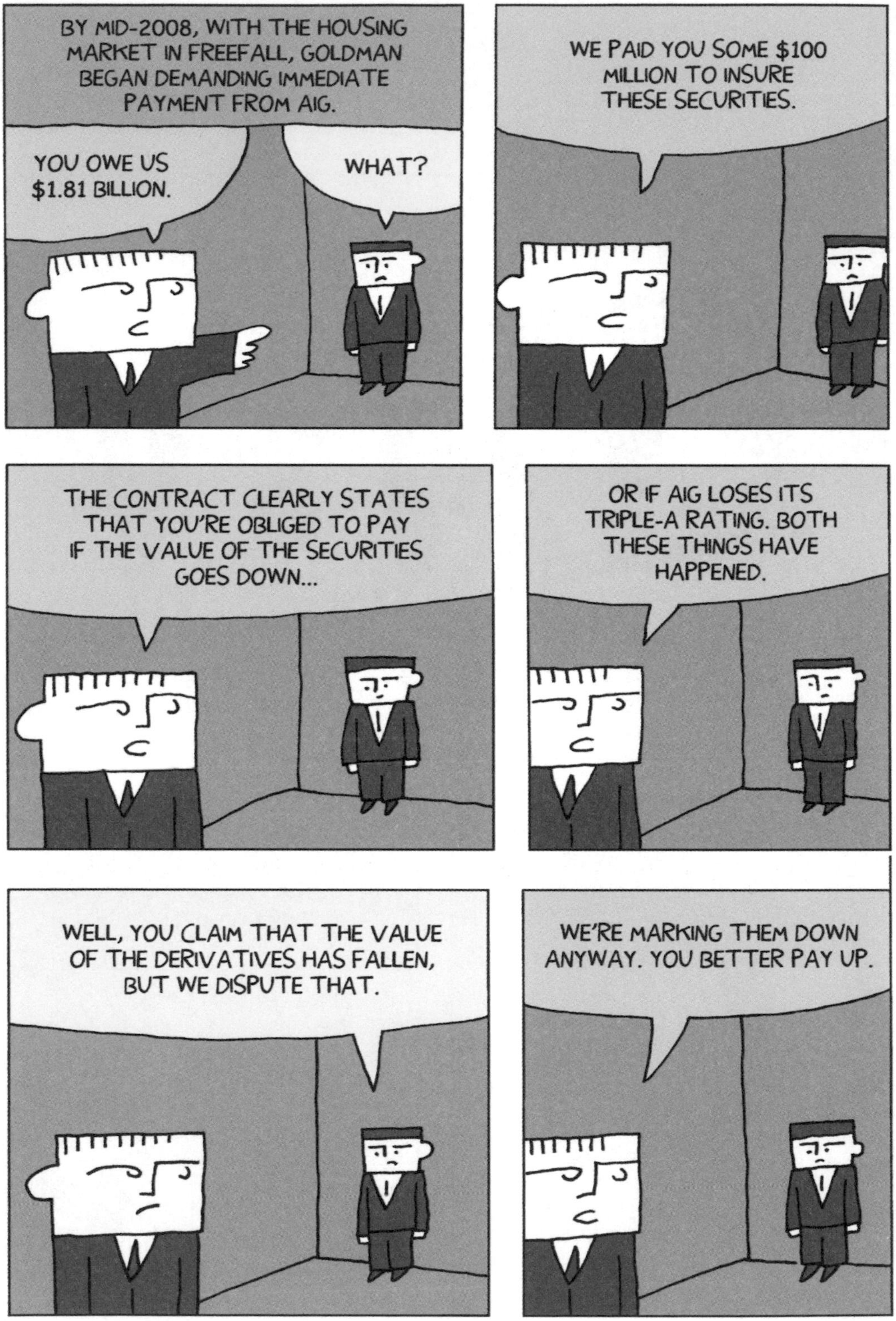
BY MID-2008, WITH THE HOUSING MARKET IN FREEFALL, GOLDMAN BEGAN DEMANDING IMMEDIATE PAYMENT FROM AIG.
YOU OWE US $1.81 BILLION.
WHAT?
WE PAID YOU SOME $100 MILLION TO INSURE THESE SECURITIES.
THE CONTRACT CLEARLY STATES THAT YOU'RE OBLIGED TO PAY IF THE VALUE OF THE SECURITIES GOES DOWN...
OR IF AIG LOSES ITS TRIPLE-A RATING. BOTH THESE THINGS HAVE HAPPENED.
WELL, YOU CLAIM THAT THE VALUE OF THE DERIVATIVES HAS FALLEN, BUT WE DISPUTE THAT.
WE'RE MARKING THEM DOWN ANYWAY. YOU BETTER PAY UP.

GOLDMAN KNEW THAT ITS PAYMENT DEMANDS COULD EASILY CAUSE AIG TO FAIL.

IT HAD FAR MORE DETAILED KNOWLEDGE OF MANY OF THE SECURITIES THAN AIG DID...

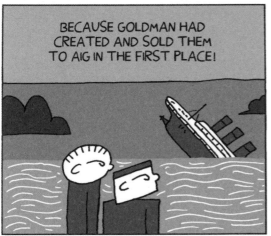

BECAUSE GOLDMAN HAD CREATED AND SOLD THEM TO AIG IN THE FIRST PLACE!

SHOULD WE WARN THE REGULATORS OR CLIENTS OF AIG ABOUT THIS SITUATION?

NO, LET'S GET OUR CASH FIRST.

AND, JUST TO BE ABSOLUTELY SURE GOLDMAN MADE MONEY OUT OF AIG'S FAILURE, IT DID SOMETHING ELSE.

WANNA MAKE SOME MONEY?

DAMN RIGHT!

INVESTOR

IT SPENT ABOUT $150 MILLION BUYING $2.5 BILLION IN CDS PROTECTION ON AIG, WHICH IT WOULD COLLECT IN THE EVENT OF AN AIG DEFAULT OR BANKRUPTCY.

WELL, I CAN'T SEE A GIANT COMPANY LIKE AIG FAILING.

BY DOING THIS, GOLDMAN CREATED A SITUATION WHERE IT WOULD PROFIT WHETHER AIG SURVIVED OR NOT.

SUCKER!

IN THE END THERE WAS A THIRD OUTCOME. THE US GOVERNMENT STEPPED IN AND SAVED AIG WITH AN $85 BILLION BAILOUT.

AS A CREDITOR, GOLDMAN COLLECTED $14 BILLION OF THIS MONEY. A NICE INJECTION OF CASH, COURTESY OF THE TAXPAYER.

NOT A BAD REWARD FOR PUSHING AIG TOWARDS BANKRUPTCY.

AIG WENT ON TO USE THE GOVERNMENT BAILOUT TO AWARD ITS TOP TRADERS AND EXECUTIVES HUNDREDS OF MILLIONS IN BONUSES.

IN THE MORALITY-FREE ZONE OF BIG FINANCE, IT SEEMS THAT TACTICS LIKE THOSE USED BY GOLDMAN SACHS ARE MUCH ADMIRED.

IT'S JUST BUSINESS.

DIDN'T GOLDMAN SACHS HAVE SOME INVOLVEMENT IN THE COLLAPSE OF GREECE AND THE EUROPEAN SOVEREIGN DEBT CRISIS?

EUROPEAN UNION RULES FORBID MEMBER COUNTRIES TO EXCEED A BUDGET DEFICIT LIMIT OF THREE PER CENT GROSS DOMESTIC PRODUCT.

TOTAL GOVERNMENT DEBT MUST NOT GO ABOVE SIXTY PER CENT OR LARGE FINES CAN BE IMPOSED.

GREECE HAS CONSTANTLY FAILED TO KEEP BELOW THE SIXTY PER CENT LIMIT...

AND IT ONLY MANAGED TO STAY BELOW THE THREE PER CENT DEFICIT CEILING BY USING BLATANT BALANCE SHEET COSMETICS.

WHAT IF WE LEFT OUT A BIG SECTION OF MILITARY SPENDING?

OK!

AT THE START OF 2002, GREECE'S DEBT MANAGERS AGREED A HUGE DEAL WITH GOLDMAN SACHS.

GOLDMAN DEVISED A WAY OF BOTH HIDING GREEK DEBT AND GIVING THE COUNTRY AN ADDITIONAL LOAN.

WE'LL JUST SWEEP IT UNDER HERE.

A COMPLICATED CROSS-CURRENCY SWAP WAS ARRANGED IN WHICH GOVERNMENT DEBT, ISSUED IN DOLLARS AND YEN...

WAS SWAPPED FOR EURO DEBT, TO BE PAID BACK LATER. THE ADDITIONAL FINANCE WAS SNUCK IN ON THIS DEAL.

ALL PERFECTLY LEGAL, WHILE BEING INVISIBLE TO THE BUREAUCRATS OF THE EUROPEAN UNION.

?

EUROSTAT

OR IF THEY DID KNOW, THEY TURNED A BLIND EYE.

I KNOW NOTHING.

EUROSTAT

THE EFFECT WAS TO MAKE GREECE LOOK MORE SOLVENT THAT IT WAS, WITH DISASTROUS CONSEQUENCES LATER.

YET ANOTHER EXAMPLE OF GOLDMAN'S SHARP PRACTICE WAS ITS ASSOCIATION WITH JOHN PAULSON (NO RELATION TO HANK PAULSON).

PAULSON, AN AMERICAN HEDGE FUND MANAGER, REALISED AT THE HEIGHT OF THE HOUSING BUBBLE WHERE THE MARKET WAS GOING.

SO HE HAND-PICKED MORTGAGE-BACKED SECURITIES HE EXPECTED TO FAIL.

THEN GOLDMAN SACHS BUNDLED THEM TOGETHER INTO AN INVESTMENT PRODUCT CALLED ABACUS.

GOLDMAN THEN SOLD ABACUS TO LUCKLESS INVESTORS, WHILE PAULSON BET AGAINST THEM.

IT'S A SURE-FIRE WINNER. YOU CAN'T LOSE.

GOSH!

THE PRODUCT DID INDEED FAIL. INVESTORS LOST MILLIONS. PAULSON MADE BILLIONS. GOLDMAN RECIEVED ABOUT $15 MILLION IN FEES.

SUCKER!

GOLDMAN WAS FINED $550 MILLION BY THE SECURITIES AND EXCHANGE COMMISSION FOR MISLEADING ITS CLIENTS.

MISLEADING IS JUST ANOTHER WORD FOR FRAUD, RIGHT?

THIS WAS A HUGE FINE, BUT PALTRY WHEN YOU CONSIDER THE COLOSSAL AMOUNTS OF MONEY SUCH FIRMS MAKE.

AND, AS OFTEN HAPPENS WITH SUCH FINANCIAL WRONGDOINGS, NOBODY WENT TO PRISON.

PRISON IS FOR LITTLE PEOPLE.

IS EVERYONE WHO WORKS IN THE FINANCIAL SECTOR CROOKED?

OF COURSE NOT, BUT THE CULTURE OF GREED MAKES IT HARD FOR AN HONEST PERSON TO PROSPER.

IN MARCH 2012, GREG SMITH, THE HEAD OF GOLDMAN SACHS' US EQUITY DERIVATIVES BUSINESS IN EUROPE, THE MIDDLE EAST, AND AFRICA, RESIGNED.

SMITH, WHO HAD WORKED FOR GOLDMAN FOR TWELVE YEARS, WROTE HIS RESIGNATION LETTER AS AN OPINION EDITORIAL FOR THE 'NEW YORK TIMES'.

THE FIRM HAS VEERED SO FAR FROM THE PLACE I JOINED RIGHT OUT OF COLLEGE THAT I CAN NO LONGER IN GOOD CONSCIENCE SAY THAT I IDENTIFY WITH WHAT IT STANDS FOR.

I AM SAD TO SAY THAT I LOOK AROUND TODAY AND SEE VIRTUALLY NO TRACE OF THE CULTURE THAT MADE ME LOVE WORKING FOR THIS FIRM FOR MANY YEARS. I NO LONGER HAVE THE PRIDE, OR THE BELIEF.

I ATTEND DERIVATIVES SALES MEETINGS WHERE NOT ONE SINGLE MINUTE IS SPENT ASKING QUESTIONS ABOUT HOW WE CAN HELP CLIENTS. IT'S PURELY ABOUT HOW WE CAN MAKE THE MOST POSSIBLE MONEY OUT OF THEM.

IT MAKES ME ILL HOW CALLOUSLY PEOPLE TALK ABOUT RIPPING THEIR CLIENTS OFF. OVER THE LAST TWELVE MONTHS I HAVE SEEN FIVE DIFFERENT MANAGING DIRECTORS REFER TO THEIR OWN CLIENTS AS 'MUPPETS'.

GOLDMAN SACHS DID NOT CAUSE THE EUROPEAN DEBT CRISIS. THE FIRM'S INVOLVEMENT WAS ONLY ONE OF A NUMBER OF ELEMENTS THAT BROUGHT THE UNGAINLY EDIFICE OF THE EU TO ITS KNEES.

BUT, WITHOUT THE GOLDMAN DEAL, GREECE'S MEMBERSHIP OF THE EU WOULD HAVE BEEN MORE DIFFICULT TO ACHIEVE, BECAUSE ITS DEBT WOULD NOT HAVE LOOKED TO BE IN DECLINE.

GREG SMITH BLAMED GOLDMAN SACHS' LACK OF ETHICS SQUARELY ON THE LEADERSHIP OF THE COMPANY.

WHEN THE HISTORY BOOKS ARE WRITTEN ABOUT GOLDMAN SACHS, THEY MAY REFLECT THAT THE CURRENT CHIEF EXECUTIVE OFFICER, LLOYD C. BLANKFEIN, AND THE PRESIDENT, GARY COHN, LOST HOLD OF THE FIRM'S CULTURE ON THEIR WATCH.

SMITH'S CRITICISMS CAN EASILY BE APPLIED TO THE FINANCIAL SYSTEM AS A WHOLE, WHERE, FREED FROM THE LEASH OF GOVERNMENT REGULATION, ENORMOUS, RAPACIOUS, SOCIALLY DESTRUCTIVE CORPORATIONS HAVE RUN AMOK.

ROAR!

HOLY SHIT!

WELL, I HEARD THE GOVERNMENT WAS BEHIND BOTH THE HOUSING BOOM AND THE FINANCIAL CRASH. I SAW IT ON FOX NEWS.

MANY OF THOSE ON THE POLITICAL RIGHT WANT TO SHIFT THE BLAME AWAY FROM THE FREE MARKET AND ONTO THE GOVERNMENT. TWO QUASI-GOVERNMENTAL ORGANISATIONS THEY BLAME IN PARTICULAR ARE KNOWN AS FANNIE MAE AND FREDDIE MAC.

THE FEDERAL NATIONAL MORTGAGE ASSOCIATION (FNMA), KNOWN AS FANNIE MAE, WAS CREATED IN 1938, AS PART OF PRESIDENT FRANKLIN D. ROOSEVELT'S EFFORT TO REVIVE THE US HOUSING MARKET IN THE WAKE OF THE GREAT DEPRESSION.

FANNIE MAE PROVIDED LOCAL BANKS WITH FEDERAL MONEY TO FINANCE MORTGAGES IN AN ATTEMPT TO RAISE LEVELS OF HOME OWNERSHIP AND AVAILABILITY OF AFFORDABLE HOUSING.

IT REMAINED PART OF THE FEDERAL BUDGET UNTIL 1968, WHEN PRESIDENT LYNDON B. JOHNSON, WHO WAS FACING A BIG DEFICIT DUE TO THE VIETNAM WAR, PRIVATISED FANNIE MAE IN ORDER TO REMOVE IT FROM THE FEDERAL BUDGET.

SO IT BECAME THIS CURIOUS BEAST, A PRIVATE COMPANY WITH SHAREHOLDERS, WHICH IN THEORY RETAINED THE SOCIAL REMIT TO HELP POOR PEOPLE BUY HOMES, YET KEPT ITS STRONG LINKS WITH GOVERNMENT.

IN 1970 THE FEDERAL GOVERNMENT AUTHORISED FANNIE MAE TO SELL PRIVATE MORTGAGES. IT ALSO CREATED THE FEDERAL HOME LOAN MORTGAGE CORPORATION (FHLMC), KNOWN AS FREDDIE MAC, TO COMPETE WITH FANNIE MAE.

OVER THE THREE DECADES BEFORE THE CRASH, FANNIE AND FREDDIE MANAGED GRADUALLY TO FREE THEMSELVES FROM REGULATORY RESTRAINTS IN PURSUIT OF PROFIT.

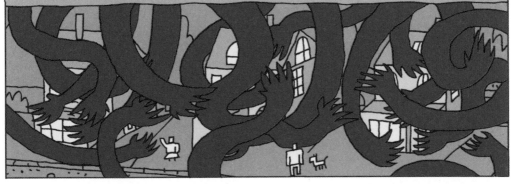

THEY GREW SO POWERFUL THAT THEY EASILY NEUTERED CONGRESSIONAL OVERSIGHT AND THE UNDERSTAFFED BODIES MEANT TO SUPERVISE THEM. THEY ACHIEVED THIS THROUGH A COMBINATION OF AGGRESSIVE LOBBYING, PATRONAGE, REVOLVING-DOOR HIRING, AND BLATANT DECEIT.

BOTH FIRMS FILLED THEIR BOARDS OF DIRECTORS WITH THE COMPLIANT AND POLITICALLY WELL-CONNECTED. THEY ALSO USED THE SAME COMPENSATION STRUCTURE THAT HAD CAUSED SO MUCH DAMAGE IN THE REST OF THE FINANCIAL SECTOR – LARGE BONUSES, BASED ON SHORT-TERM PERFORMANCE.

IN 2006, US REGULATORS FILED 101 CIVIL CHARGES AGAINST FANNIE MAE'S CHIEF EXECUTIVE FRANKLIN RAINES, CHIEF FINANCIAL OFFICER J. TIMOTHY HOWARD, AND THE FORMER CONTROLLER LEANNE G. SPENCER. THE THREE WERE ACCUSED OF MANIPULATING THE FIRM'S EARNINGS IN ORDER TO MAXIMISE THEIR BONUSES.

SETTLEMENTS FOR ALL THREE EXECUTIVES ALLOWED THEM TO KEEP THE MAJORITY OF THEIR BONUSES, AND NONE OF THEM HAD TO ADMIT GUILT. FANNIE MAE PAID A $400 MILLION CORPORATE FINE. NO CRIMINAL CASES WERE BROUGHT IN THIS SCANDAL.

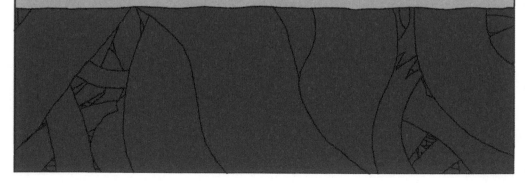

THE COLLAPSE OF THE HOUSING BUBBLE HIT FANNIE AND FREDDIE HARD. IN SEPTEMBER 2008, HANK PAULSON AND THE US GOVERNMENT STEPPED IN AND TOOK OVER BOTH FIRMS, POURING IN THE USUAL TAXPAYERS' BILLIONS TO COVER THE COMPANIES' LOSSES.

DID FANNIE AND FREDDIE CAUSE THE FINANCIAL CRASH? THEY DID CONTRIBUTE, BUT NO MORE THAN ANY OF THE OTHER PLAYERS. THEY WERE LATE ENTERING THE GAME, DUE PARTLY TO THE EARLIER ACCOUNTING FRAUD SCANDAL.

WHAT DROVE FANNIE AND FREDDIE TO LOWER THEIR CREDIT STANDARDS, AND INCREASE THE NUMBER OF LOANS THEY BOUGHT, WAS NOT POLITICAL PRESSURE FROM DO-GOODER DEMOCRATS, BUT THE STRAIGHT-FORWARD SEARCH FOR PROFITS.

THERE IS NOTHING WRONG WITH THAT IN ITSELF. A COMPANY HAS TO MAKE A PROFIT TO SURVIVE. FANNIE AND FREDDIE WERE NO WORSE THAN ANY OTHER FIRM INVOLVED IN THE CRISIS. TO SINGLE THEM OUT IS TO NOT UNDERSTAND THE CAUSES OF THE DISASTER. THESE CAUSES INCLUDE THE COLLAPSE OF ETHICS, POOR REGULATION, AND THE SPREAD OF TOXIC INCENTIVES FOR INDIVIDUALS THROUGHOUT THE FINANCIAL SECTOR...

ALL CONVERGING TO CAUSE COLOSSAL DAMAGE. THE EVENTS LEADING UP TO THE 2008 CRISIS SHOULD HAVE DESTROYED THE FANTASY THAT AN UNREGULATED FINANCIAL INDUSTRY WILL NATURALLY CHANNEL MONEY TO ITS BEST USES, OR THAT BANKERS' CONCERN FOR THEIR REPUTATIONS WOULD PREVENT THEM FROM PLACING THEIR INSTITUTIONS OR CUSTOMERS AT RISK. SADLY, THIS HAS NOT PROVED TO BE THE CASE.

THERE IS STILL A STRONG BELIEF ON THE RIGHT THAT THE FREE MARKET CAN SOLVE ALL PROBLEMS AND THAT THE FINANCIAL CRISIS WAS CAUSED BY THE LAST VESTIGES OF REGULATION AND GOVERNMENT INTERFERENCE. THEY CLAIM THAT ONLY WITH THE TOTAL REPEAL OF INTERVENTIONIST LAWS AND REGULATORY AGENCIES CAN MARKETS FIND THEIR TRUE VALUE, SO THAT PEOPLE CAN PROSPER.

THIS CLEARLY FLIES IN THE FACE OF REALITY. IF THE LAST THIRTY YEARS HAVE SHOWN US ANYTHING, IT IS THAT FREE MARKETS LEAD NOT TO PERSONAL FREEDOM, BUT TO CORPORATE FREEDOM — A FREEDOM THAT HAS BEEN EMBRACED COUNTLESS TIMES IN THE PAST TO POLLUTE, STEAL, AND OPPRESS.

IN CONGRESSIONAL HEARINGS IN 2008, BEFORE A HOUSE COMMITTEE, ALAN GREENSPAN FAMOUSLY TESTIFIED THAT HE HAD FOUND A FLAW IN HIS ECONOMIC THINKING.

I MADE A MISTAKE IN PRESUMING THAT THE SELF-INTEREST OF ORGANISATIONS, SPECIFICALLY BANKS AND OTHERS, WAS SUCH THAT THEY WERE BEST CAPABLE OF PROTECTING THEIR OWN SHAREHOLDERS AND THEIR EQUITY IN THE FIRMS.

YOU FOUND THAT YOUR VIEW OF THE WORLD, YOUR IDEOLOGY WAS NOT RIGHT; IT WAS NOT WORKING.

THAT'S PRECISELY THE REASON I WAS SHOCKED, BECAUSE I'D BEEN GOING FOR FORTY YEARS OR MORE WITH VERY CONSIDERABLE EVIDENCE THAT IT WAS WORKING EXCEPTIONALLY WELL.

DID GREENSPAN GENUINELY BELIEVE THAT AN UNREGULATED FINANCIAL SECTOR PURSUING SELF-INTEREST WOULD LEAD THE US ECONOMY TO A STABLE AND OPTIMAL EQUILIBRIUM?

HE DID, AND HE HELD FAST TO THESE BELIEFS LONG PAST THE POINT WHERE THE EVIDENCE SHOULD HAVE ALERTED HIM TO THE TRUTH.

SELFISHNESS IS NOT A VIRTUE TO BE EMBRACED. SELF-INTEREST DOES NOT WORK TO BRING ABOUT HUMAN HAPPINESS ON A GLOBAL SCALE ANY MORE EFFICIENTLY THAN IT ACHIEVES IT FOR PEOPLE ON THE SMALL INTERPERSONAL LEVEL WHERE WE ALL LIVE OUR LIVES.

IT'S ALL ABOUT ME

THE DETAILS OF GREENSPAN'S MENTOR AYN RAND'S OWN LIFE DEMONSTRATE THIS LAST POINT VERY EFFECTIVELY.

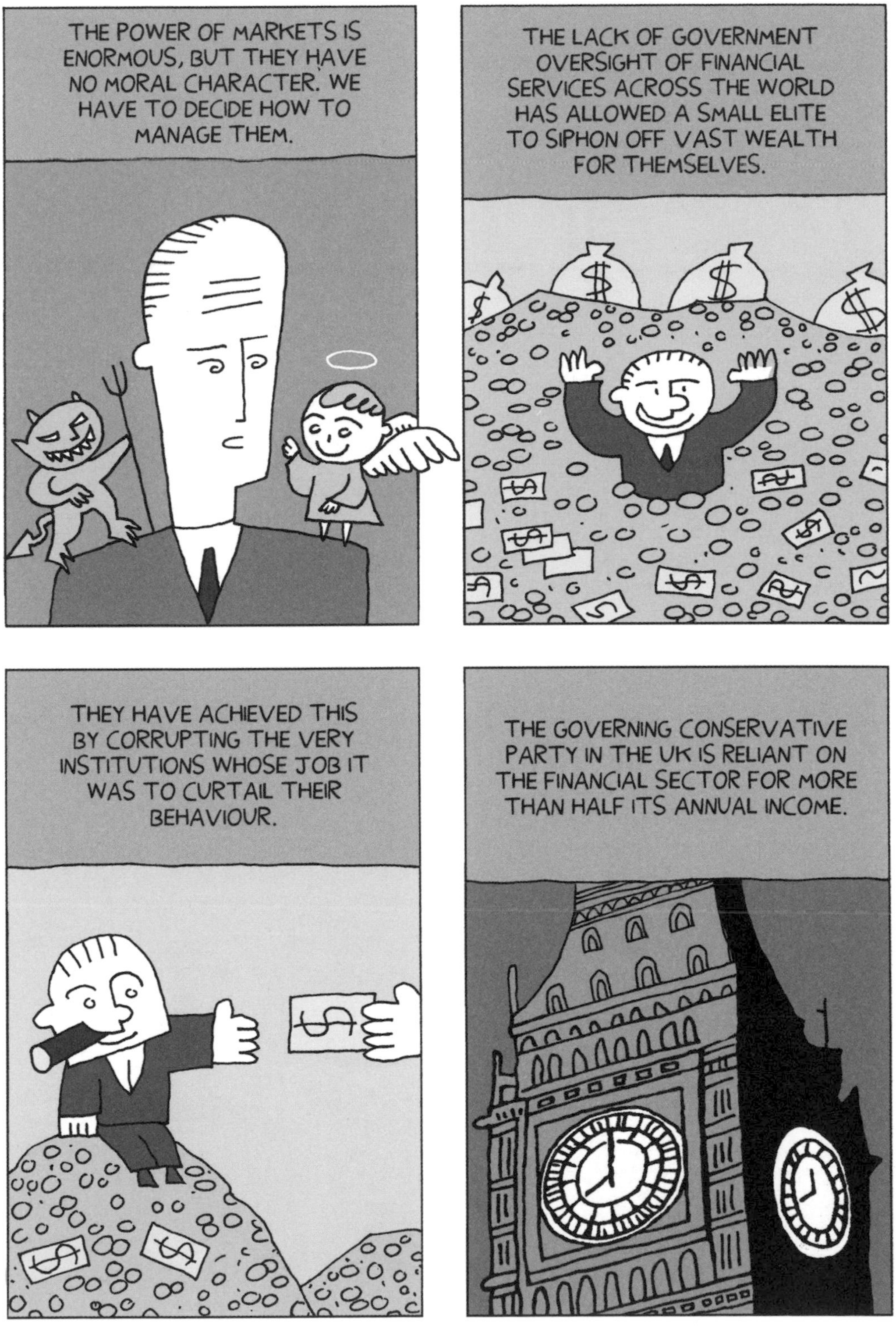
THE POWER OF MARKETS IS ENORMOUS, BUT THEY HAVE NO MORAL CHARACTER. WE HAVE TO DECIDE HOW TO MANAGE THEM.
THE LACK OF GOVERNMENT OVERSIGHT OF FINANCIAL SERVICES ACROSS THE WORLD HAS ALLOWED A SMALL ELITE TO SIPHON OFF VAST WEALTH FOR THEMSELVES.
THEY HAVE ACHIEVED THIS BY CORRUPTING THE VERY INSTITUTIONS WHOSE JOB IT WAS TO CURTAIL THEIR BEHAVIOUR.
THE GOVERNING CONSERVATIVE PARTY IN THE UK IS RELIANT ON THE FINANCIAL SECTOR FOR MORE THAN HALF ITS ANNUAL INCOME.

IN THE US, THE FINANCIAL SECTOR INVESTED MORE THAN $55 BILLION IN POLITICAL INFLUENCE OVER THE TEN-YEAR PERIOD FROM 1998 TO 2008.

ABOUT 55 PER CENT WENT TO THE REPUBLICANS AND 45 PER CENT WENT TO THE DEMOCRATS. THE DEMOCRATS TOOK MORE THAN HALF OF THE FINANCIAL SECTOR'S 2008 ELECTION CYCLE CONTRIBUTIONS.

THE INDUSTRY SPENT EVEN MORE — $3.3 BILLION — ON OFFICIALLY REGISTERED LOBBYISTS DURING THE SAME PERIOD.

TOP WALL STREET INDIVIDUALS ARE ROUTINELY APPOINTED TO KEY POSITIONS WITHIN GOVERNMENT, RETURNING TO THE PRIVATE SECTOR, OR TO ACADEMIA, WHEN THEIR TERM ENDS, THEN OFTEN GIVEN A FURTHER GOVERNMENT APPOINTMENT A FEW YEARS LATER.

NO REGULA-TION.

THIS REVOLVING-DOOR CULTURE BLURS THE LINE BETWEEN GOVERNMENT AND BIG BANKS SO COMPLETELY THAT THEIR NEEDS AND VIEWS ARE INDISTINGUISHABLE.

WHEN ALMOST ALL THE FEDERAL REGULATORS OF AN INDUSTRY SHARE A SYMPATHETIC WORLD VIEW WITH THAT INDUSTRY...

WE DON'T WANT TO STIFLE CREATIVITY.

IT CREATES A SITUATION THAT LEADS TO GROUP-THINK, NON-EXISTENT PROSECUTION, AND WEAK SAFEGUARDS.

OOPS!

IT IS NO SURPRISE THAT THE BANKING REFORMS PROPOSED BY THE US GOVERNMENT HAVE BEEN WATERED DOWN INTO A FORM THAT FAVOURS GIANT BANKS OVER SMALL ONES.

GOLDMAN SACHS

ACROSS THE WESTERN WORLD THE FINANCIAL SECTOR HAS ACHIEVED UNDUE INFLUENCE OVER GOVERNMENTS.

IT HAS MANAGED TO UNDERMINE DEMOCRACY AND TURN A PRIVATE SECTOR CRISIS INTO A PUBLIC ONE.

SAVAGE CUTS ARE NEEDED IN ORDER TO REDUCE THE SIZE OF THE DEBT.

NEARLY EVERYWHERE, THE GENERAL PUBLIC HAS BEEN PRESENTED WITH THE BILL FOR BANKING INCOMPETENCE AND CRIMINALITY.

I CAN'T PAY THIS. IT'S TRILLIONS.

BILL

IN BRITAIN, THE RIGHT-WING COALITION GOVERNMENT HAS PRESSED ON WITH AUSTERITY MEASURES, DESPITE ALL EVIDENCE THAT SUCH POLICIES CAN ONLY SLOW AN ECONOMY'S PATH OUT OF A RECESSION.

STOP!

THIS IS BECAUSE, FOR THE POLITICAL RIGHT, ECONOMIC RECOVERY IS ONLY A SECONDARY AIM. THE MAIN PURPOSE OF THE AUSTERITY PROGRAMME IS TO DISMANTLE THE WELFARE STATE, BRING DOWN WAGES, AND FULLY MARKETISE THE ECONOMY.

THE SHRINKING AWAY OF THE STATE IS A LONG-HELD LIBERTARIAN DREAM, BUT ONE THAT CAN ONLY CONTINUE THE PROCESS OF HANDING POWER OVER TO UNACCOUNTABLE CORPORATIONS. A PROSPECT EVEN WORSE THAN STATE TYRANNY, BECAUSE, IN DEMOCRATIC GOVERNMENT AT LEAST, THE PUBLIC HAS SOME KIND OF ROLE.

PART THREE

THE AGE OF SELFISHNESS

AFTER THE 2008 FINANCIAL CRISIS, GOVERNMENTS WERE QUICK TO RECAPITALISE AND ADD LIQUIDITY TO THE BROKEN BANKING SYSTEM. THE POOR AND MIDDLE CLASSES HAVE HAD TO PAY FOR THE MISTAKES OF THE RICH, AND THE RESULTS HAVE BEEN DEVASTATING.

THE CONSEQUENCES WERE FELT AROUND THE WORLD. IN 2009 SOME 47 TO 84 MILLION PEOPLE IN DEVELOPING COUNTRIES WERE THOUGHT TO HAVE FALLEN INTO, OR BECOME TRAPPED IN, POVERTY, AS A RESULT OF THE FINANCIAL CRISIS.

A FURTHER 120 MILLION PEOPLE WHO WERE LIVING JUST ABOVE THE POVERTY LINE WERE PUT AT RISK OF FALLING INTO EXTREME DEPRIVATION.

POVERTY

IN THE DEVELOPED WORLD, THERE WAS A SIGNIFICANT DETERIORATION IN CHILD WELLBEING IN AREAS THAT INCLUDE HEALTH AND SAFETY, EDUCATION, HOUSING, AND ENVIRONMENT.

PUBLIC LIBRARY

CLOSED

SPAIN WAS PARTICULARLY HARD-HIT BY THE CRISIS. MORE THAN 2.2 MILLION CHILDREN ARE ESTIMATED TO HAVE FALLEN BELOW THE POVERTY LINE, WITH MANY FAMILIES HAVING TO CUT DOWN ON BASIC NECESSITIES.

WHAT'S FOR DINNER, MUM?

ER...

THE LACK OF EMPATHY SHOWN BY PEOPLE ON THE POLITICAL RIGHT TOWARDS THOSE WHO ARE DISADVANTAGED OR DIFFERENT FROM THEMSELVES IS AT THE HEART OF THE GULF THAT SEPARATES LIBERALS FROM CONSERVATIVES.

CORPORATIONS AND THE SUPER-RICH ARE BEST MOTIVATED BY MORE MONEY.

THE POLITICAL LEFT AND RIGHT DO NOT SHARE THE SAME VALUES. THE MORAL SYSTEMS EACH SIDE HAS ARE BASED ON DIFFERENT PHILOSOPHIES. TO LIBERALS, MUCH OF CONSERVATIVE POLICY APPEARS UNJUST.

THE POOR AND ORDINARY ARE BEST MOTIVATED BY LESS MONEY.

RESEARCH SHOWS CONSERVATIVES ARE COMFORTABLE WITH INEQUALITY. THEY ARE QUICK TO JUDGE OTHERS AND HAVE LITTLE PROBLEM DISMISSING ANY SCIENCE THAT RUNS COUNTER TO THEIR BELIEFS, NO MATTER WHAT THE EVIDENCE IS, OR HOW WELL ARGUED.

HELP!

WHEREAS LIBERALS TEND TO BE MORE EMPATHETIC, SEE MORE COMPLEXITY IN THE WORLD, AND ARE MORE LIKELY TO CHANGE THEIR OPINIONS WHEN PRESENTED WITH EVIDENCE THAT THEY ARE WRONG.

THE CONCEPT OF A LEFT-RIGHT DIVIDE IN POLITICS ORIGINATED IN THE FRENCH REVOLUTION, NOT MUCH MORE THAN 200 YEARS AGO. YET THIS SPATIAL ARRANGEMENT DOES SEEM TO REFLECT A DEEP TRUTH ABOUT HUMAN PSYCHOLOGY.

THERE IS NOW A LARGE BODY OF EVIDENCE SHOWING THAT ON EACH SIDE OF THE POLITICAL DIVIDE PEOPLE TEND TO PROCESS INFORMATION IN DIFFERENT WAYS, RESULTING IN A DIVERGENCE OF PSYCHOLOGICAL TRAITS.

THESE TRAITS DON'T JUST LEAD TO CONTRASTING IDEOLOGIES, BUT TO DIFFERENT LIFESTYLE CHOICES: IN LEISURE, CLOTHING, RELATIONSHIPS, AND CAREERS. THEY POWERFULLY SHAPE OUR LIVES, ALL THE WAY DOWN TO THE STUFF WE LEAVE LYING AROUND AT HOME OR AT WORK.

IN A US STUDY OF SELF-IDENTIFIED CONSERVATIVES AND LIBERALS, RESEARCHERS EXAMINED THE LIVING SPACES AND OFFICES OF PARTICIPANTS. WHAT THEY FOUND WAS THAT THE BEDROOMS OF CONSERVATIVES TENDED TO INCLUDE MORE ORGANISATIONAL ITEMS, SUCH AS CALENDARS AND STAMPS.

THESE BEDROOMS WERE MORE LIKELY TO CONTAIN HOUSEHOLD CLEANING AND MENDING ACCESSORIES, SUCH AS LAUNDRY BASKETS, IRONS AND IRONING BOARDS. CONSERVATIVE BEDROOMS WERE NEATER, CLEANER, FRESHER, MORE ORGANISED AND WELL LIT.

DECORATIONS WERE OF A CONVENTIONAL NATURE: SPORTS PARAPHERNALIA AND FLAGS, ESPECIALLY AMERICAN FLAGS. CONSERVATIVE OFFICES WERE LESS STYLISH AND LESS COMFORTABLE THAN THOSE USED BY LIBERALS.

THE BEDROOMS USED BY LIBERALS CONTAINED A GREATER NUMBER OF BOOKS, INCLUDING BOOKS ON TRAVEL, ETHNIC ISSUES, FEMINISM, AND MUSIC. THERE WAS ALSO A LARGER VARIETY OF TYPES OF MUSIC, INCLUDING WORLD MUSIC, FOLK, CLASSICAL AND ROCK.

THEY CONTAINED MORE ART SUPPLIES, STATIONERY, MAPS, TRAVEL DOCUMENTS, AND CULTURAL MEMORABILIA. LIBERAL OFFICES WERE MORE DISTINCTIVE AND COLOURFUL THAN CONSERVATIVE OFFICES.

THERE IS A WIDELY ACCEPTED SCALE USED BY PSYCHOLOGISTS TO MEASURE THE FIVE TRAITS THAT CHARACTERISE THE HUMAN PERSONALITY.

THE FIVE ARE: OPENNESS TO EXPERIENCE, CONSCIENTIOUSNESS, EXTRAVERSION, AGREEABLENESS, AND NEUROTICISM. WE ALL POSSESS THESE TRAITS TO A GREATER OR LESSER DEGREE.

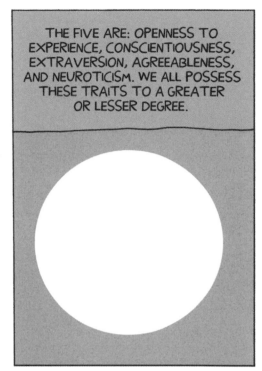

THESE ASPECTS OF OUR PERSONALITY SHOW UP WHEN WE ARE VERY YOUNG AND HARDLY CHANGE OVER OUR LIFETIME.

THE TWO TRAITS WHERE LIBERALS AND CONSERVATIVES DIFFER THE MOST ARE CONSCIENTIOUSNESS AND OPENNESS TO EXPERIENCE. LIBERALS CONSISTENTLY RATE HIGHER ON OPENNESS, AND THIS SEEMS TO BE TRUE ACROSS ALL CULTURES.

LAZY SLOB!

NARROW-MINDED BIGOT!

OPENNESS IS A BROAD PERSONALITY TRAIT THAT COVERS EVERYTHING FROM INTELLECTUAL FLEXIBILITY AND CURIOSITY TO AN ENJOYMENT OF THE ARTS AND CREATIVITY.

LIBERALS ARE RISK-TAKERS. THEY ARE EXPERIMENTAL IN THEIR LIFESTYLE CHOICES AND SELF-EXPRESSION. THEY ARE TOLERANT OF DIFFERENT PERSPECTIVES AND VALUES.

CONSERVATIVES RATE HIGHER ON CONSCIENTIOUSNESS. THEY PRIZE HARD WORK, ORDERLINESS AND STRUCTURE. THEY LIKE TO STICK TO A PREDICTABLE SCHEDULE AND ARE PUNCTUAL.

CONSERVATIVES ARE GOAL-ORIENTATED AND COMPETENT. BOTH GROUPS SCORE AROUND THE SAME ON AGREEABLENESS, BECAUSE LIBERALS VALUE EMPATHY, WHILE THOSE ON THE RIGHT EMPHASISE POLITENESS.

AFTER YOU!

NO, AFTER YOU!

LIBERALS LIKE TO THINK IN CHALLENGING WAYS. THEY ENJOY COMPLEX PROBLEMS. FOR THEM, IT IS NOT A DIFFICULTY IF THINGS ARE ILL-DEFINED OR UNRESOLVED.

CONSERVATIVES ARE THE OPPOSITE. THEY ARE MORE LIKELY TO CATEGORISE AND DIVIDE PEOPLE INTO EITHER GOOD OR BAD. IN THE CONSERVATIVE WORLD THERE ARE NO GREY AREAS, ONLY THE BLACK AND WHITE OF CERTAINTY.

THIS CREATES A CLASH OF REALITIES. CONSERVATIVES ARE RESISTANT TO CHANGE. THEY HAVE A NEED FOR STABILITY AND THE DESIRE TO MANAGE FEAR AND THREAT.

GODDAMN FAGS!

TENSION ARISES BETWEEN THE TWO GROUPS, BECAUSE LIBERALS ARE THE PEOPLE MOST LIKELY TO GENERATE THAT DANGEROUS CHANGE IN THE SOCIAL, ARTISTIC, AND SCIENTIFIC ARENAS. AND THIS IS NOT SOMETHING CONSERVATIVES WANT TO SEE.

YOU'RE DESTROYING EVERYTHING.

I'M TRYING TO BUILD A BETTER WORLD.

MANY CONSERVATIVE PERSONALITY TRAITS CAN APPEAR TO BE EXTREMELY NEGATIVE.

BUT THEY DO HAVE QUALITIES WHICH ARE POSITIVE IN THE RIGHT CONTEXT.

PATRIOTISM, DECISIVENESS, AND LOYALTY TO FRIENDS AND ALLIES.

A LIBERAL'S ABILITY TO CONSIDER THE COMPLEXITY OF AN ISSUE CAN LOOK LIKE WEAKNESS TO A CONSERVATIVE.

WHEN YOU HAVE BACKED A LIBERAL INTO A CORNER, IF HE DOESN'T START CRYING, HE'LL SAY IT'S A COMPLICATED ISSUE.

ANN COULTER. POLITICAL COMMENTATOR.

LOVING AMERICA IS TOO SIMPLE AN EMOTION. CONSERVATIVES MAY NOT GRASP NUANCE, BUT WE'RE PRETTY GOOD AT GRASPING TREASON.

THESE VERY DIFFERENT PERSONALITY TRAITS MAY BE USEFUL TO US AS A SPECIES.

IN A TIME OF WAR, WHEN DECISIVE ACTION IS NEEDED, THERE IS LITTLE ROOM FOR MORAL QUALMS OR HESITATION.

AN ENEMY'S POINT OF VIEW DOES NOT NEED TO BE UNDERSTOOD.

THEIR FEELINGS DO NOT NEED TO BE EMPATHISED WITH.

TO WIN A WAR IT HELPS TO BE DEDICATED TO THE CAUSE, DISINCLINED TO COMPROMISE, AND CERTAIN THE ENEMY IS WRONG.

ALL CONSERVATIVE TRAITS, RATHER THAN LIBERAL ONES.

COWARD!

ER!

IS IT POSSIBLE FOR PEOPLE ON THE LEFT TO MOVE TO THE POLITICAL RIGHT? WELL, ALL THE EVIDENCE SUGGESTS THAT, UNDER CONDITIONS OF STRESS, LIBERALS BECOME MORE CONSERVATIVE IN THEIR VIEWS.

IN A STUDY AT THE UNIVERSITY OF ILLINOIS IN CHICAGO, LIBERALS AND CONSERVATIVES WERE ASKED QUESTIONS ABOUT A SCENARIO WHERE VARIOUS GROUPS HAD CONTRACTED AIDS IN DIFFERENT WAYS.

THREE OF THESE GROUPS HAD GOT THE ILLNESS FROM BLOOD TRANSFUSIONS OR VIA A LONG-TERM PARTNER WHO WAS CHEATING ON THEM, OR BEFORE IT WAS WIDELY KNOWN THAT AIDS WAS SEXUALLY TRANSMITTED.

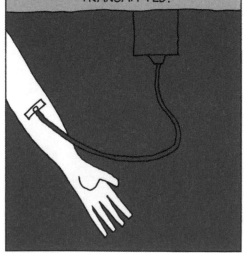

THE FOURTH GROUP WAS DIFFERENT, BECAUSE THESE INDIVIDUALS HAD CONTRACTED AIDS BY PRACTISING UNSAFE SEX WHILE BEING FULLY AWARE OF THE RISKS.

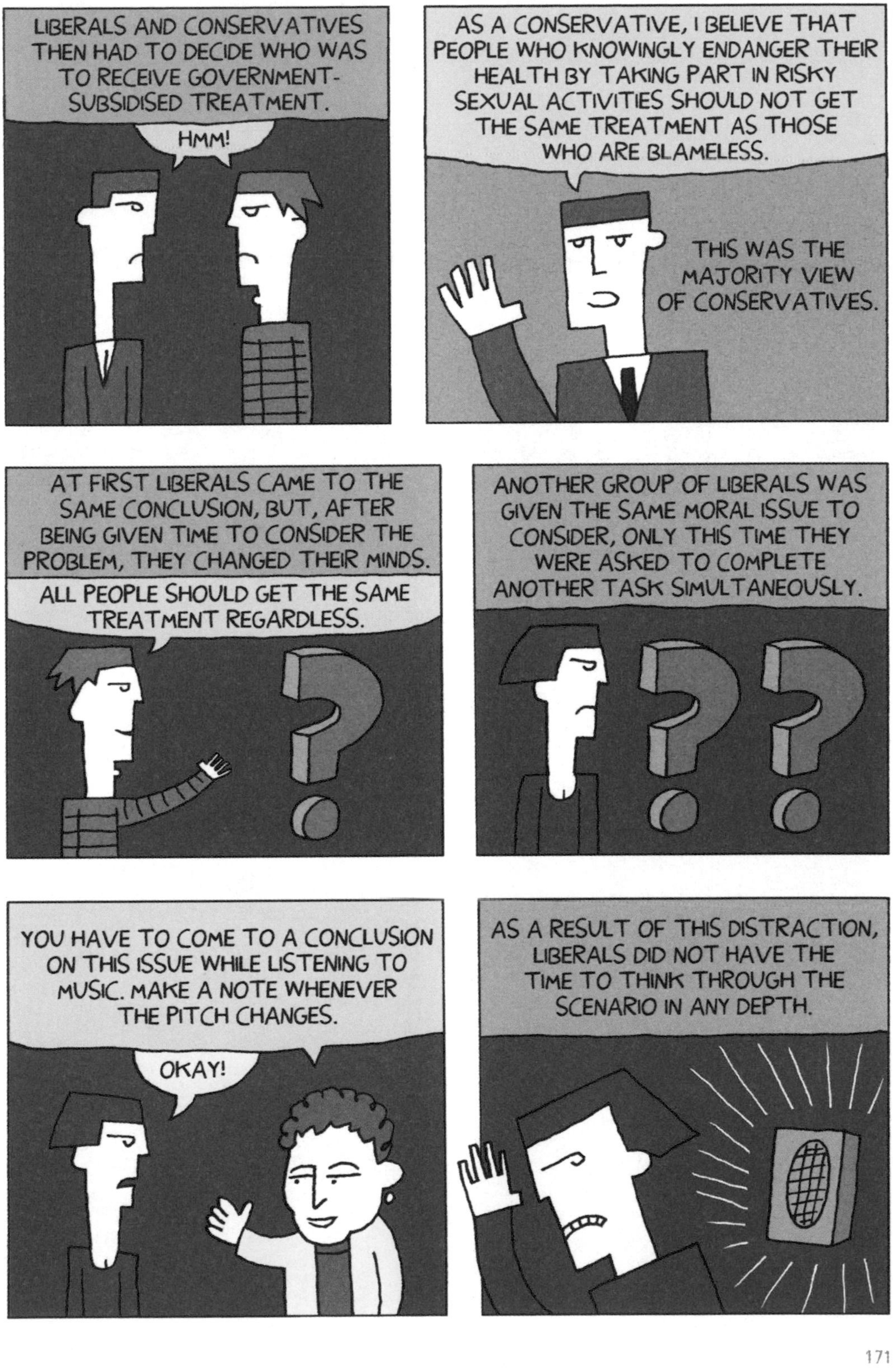
LIBERALS AND CONSERVATIVES THEN HAD TO DECIDE WHO WAS TO RECEIVE GOVERNMENT-SUBSIDISED TREATMENT.
HMM!
AS A CONSERVATIVE, I BELIEVE THAT PEOPLE WHO KNOWINGLY ENDANGER THEIR HEALTH BY TAKING PART IN RISKY SEXUAL ACTIVITIES SHOULD NOT GET THE SAME TREATMENT AS THOSE WHO ARE BLAMELESS.
THIS WAS THE MAJORITY VIEW OF CONSERVATIVES.
AT FIRST LIBERALS CAME TO THE SAME CONCLUSION, BUT, AFTER BEING GIVEN TIME TO CONSIDER THE PROBLEM, THEY CHANGED THEIR MINDS.
ALL PEOPLE SHOULD GET THE SAME TREATMENT REGARDLESS.
ANOTHER GROUP OF LIBERALS WAS GIVEN THE SAME MORAL ISSUE TO CONSIDER, ONLY THIS TIME THEY WERE ASKED TO COMPLETE ANOTHER TASK SIMULTANEOUSLY.
YOU HAVE TO COME TO A CONCLUSION ON THIS ISSUE WHILE LISTENING TO MUSIC. MAKE A NOTE WHENEVER THE PITCH CHANGES.
OKAY!
AS A RESULT OF THIS DISTRACTION, LIBERALS DID NOT HAVE THE TIME TO THINK THROUGH THE SCENARIO IN ANY DEPTH.

THERE WAS THEN NO REAL DIFFERENCE BETWEEN LIBERALS AND CONSERVATIVES. BOTH GROUPS WERE EQUALLY HARSH IN THEIR JUDGEMENT OF WHO THEY CONSIDERED TO BE CULPABLE AIDS SUFFERERS.

WHAT THIS STUDY, AND OTHERS LIKE IT, SUGGESTS IS THAT UNDER STRESS THE ABILITY TO CARRY OUT COMPLEX THINKING IS OVERRIDDEN. IN SUCH SITUATIONS EVEN LIBERALS WILL ACT INSTINCTIVELY, FOLLOW QUICK IMPULSES, AND BLAME OTHERS FOR THEIR FAILINGS.

BECAUSE OF TERRORISM WE NEED TO SCRAP OUR HUMAN RIGHTS.

APPLY ANXIETY OR FEAR AND LIBERALS WILL BE AS LIKELY AS CONSERVATIVES TO SUPPORT DECISIVE LEADERS AND THE REMOVAL OF CIVIL LIBERTIES.

THIS EXPLAINS WHY SCARE-MONGERING IS SUCH AN EFFECTIVE TACTIC FOR CONSERVATIVE POLITICIANS AND THEIR MEDIA OUTLETS. THE POLITICAL RIGHT DOES WELL IN A CLIMATE OF FEAR.

BLOODY IMMIGRANTS!

SEVERAL STUDIES HAVE SHOWN THAT CONSERVATIVES HAVE STRONGER REACTIONS TO DISTURBING NOISES AND IMAGES THAN LIBERALS. THEY ARE MORE LIKELY TO INTERPRET FACES AS THREATENING, AND OVERALL ARE MORE SENSITIVE TO SIGNS OF DANGER THAN ARE THEIR LIBERAL COUNTERPARTS.

THIS DOES NOT MEAN CONSERVATIVES ARE PARANOID. NONE OF THE PERSONALITY TRAITS REVEALED BY RESEARCH ARE OUTSIDE THE NORMAL PARAMETERS OF HUMAN PSYCHOLOGY.

I'M NOT PARANOID. WHO'S BEEN SAYING THAT ABOUT ME?

THE STABILITY DELIVERED BY THE CONSERVATIVE VALUES OF ORDER AND STRUCTURE CAN WORK WELL AS A USEFUL CORRECTIVE FOR HUMAN SOCIETY DURING CHAOTIC TIMES.

BUT THE DARK SIDE OF THESE VALUES IS THAT THE POLITICAL RIGHT WILL INSTINCTIVELY RESIST CHANGES, EVEN IF THOSE CHANGES ARE BENEFICIAL TO THEMSELVES...

FACTS ARE STUPID THINGS.

ACTUAL RONALD REAGAN QUOTE.

WHICH IS WHY LIBERALS ARE OFTEN SHOCKED TO FIND THAT THEIR WELL-REASONED AND FACTUALLY SUPPORTED ARGUMENTS ARE SIMPLY DISMISSED OR EVEN VICIOUSLY ATTACKED BY THE POLITICAL RIGHT.

BUT LOOK AT ALL THE EVIDENCE.

I DON'T CARE ABOUT EVIDENCE.

CONSERVATIVES SEEM TO HAVE A GIFT FOR BLOCKING OUT FACTS THAT THREATEN THEIR WORLD VIEW. WE SEE THIS IN THEIR INTENSE RESISTANCE TO THE EVIDENCE FOR CLIMATE CHANGE AND EVOLUTION.

BECAUSE OF THIS, IT WILL PERHAPS COME AS NO SURPRISE THAT THERE ARE MORE LIBERALS IN SCIENCE THAN CONSERVATIVES.

THE COMPLEXITIES AND AMBIGUITIES OF RESEARCH, THE CHANCE TO EXPLORE NOVEL IDEAS AND IMPROVE SOCIETY, ARE ALL QUALITIES THAT ARE MORE ATTRACTIVE TO LIBERALS THAN TO THOSE ON THE RIGHT.

IN A 2006 SURVEY OF 1,400 PROFESSORS WORKING IN NEARLY ALL TYPES OF INSTITUTIONS, 51 PER CENT OF ACADEMICS DESCRIBED THEMSELVES AS DEMOCRATS, AND 35.3 PER CENT AS INDEPENDENT, OF WHICH THE MAJORITY CONSIDERED THEMSELVES LEFT-LEANING. ONLY 13 PER CENT CONSIDERED THEMSELVES ON THE RIGHT AND REPUBLICAN.

ARE YOU CONSERVATIVE OR LIBERAL?

I'D LIKE TO SPEND TIME CONSIDERING THIS IMPORTANT QUESTION.

THIS RESULT WAS REINFORCED BY A 2009 SURVEY OF THE AMERICAN ASSOCIATION FOR THE ADVANCEMENT OF SCIENCE, WHICH FOUND THAT 55 PER CENT WERE LIBERAL, 33 PER CENT WERE INDEPENDENT, WHILE ONLY ONE PER CENT WERE REPUBLICAN.

AND YOU?

I'M A PATRIOT.

IT HAS BEEN A LONG-HELD VIEW OF THE POLITICAL RIGHT, ESPECIALLY IN THE US, THAT HIGHER EDUCATION IS DOMINATED BY LIBERALS BECAUSE COLLEGES AND UNIVERSITIES INDOCTRINATE THE YOUNG.

INDOCTRINATION
AHEAD

THIS OPINION IS WRONG. THE GROUNDWORK FOR OUR POLITICAL VIEWS IS LAID DOWN YEARS BEFORE WE CHOOSE A CAREER PATH.

RESEARCH STARTED IN 1969 BY THE UNIVERSITY OF CALIFORNIA AT BERKELEY SUGGESTS THAT POLITICAL ORIENTATION IS SET DOWN VERY EARLY IN LIFE.

THE STUDY TRACKED CHILDREN OVER TWENTY YEARS IN AN ATTEMPT TO DISCOVER IF CHILDHOOD PERSONALITY TRAITS WERE LINKED TO LATER ADULT POLITICAL PERSUASIONS. PRE-SCHOOLERS WERE FIRST ASSESSED AT AGES THREE AND FOUR, THEN AGAIN AT THE AGE OF TWENTY-ONE.

I NEED TO ASK YOU A BATTERY OF POLITICAL QUESTIONS.

OKAY!

CHILDREN WHO IN LATER LIFE BECAME CONSERVATIVE WERE NOTED TO BE UNCOMFORTABLE WITH UNCERTAINTY, SUSCEPTIBLE TO A SENSE OF GUILT, AND RIGIDIFYING WHEN EXPERIENCING DURESS, WHILE THEIR LIBERAL COUNTERPARTS WERE DESCRIBED AS AUTONOMOUS, EXPRESSIVE, AND SELF-RELIANT.

CONSERVATIVE CHILDREN TENDED TO OVER-CONTROL THEIR ENVIRONMENT, WHILE LIBERALS WERE HAPPY TO UNDER-CONTROL IT. HERE WE SEE ONCE MORE THE SPLIT IN HUMAN PERSONALITY: THE NEED TO MAINTAIN ORDER, TO PROTECT AND SERVE, VERSUS THE WISH TO GENERATE NEW IDEAS AND CHALLENGE THE STATUS QUO.

YOU'VE SAID MUCH ABOUT THE DARK SIDE OF CONSERVATISM, BUT LITTLE ABOUT THE NEGATIVE ASPECTS OF LIBERALISM.

WHAT HAVE YOU GOT TO SAY ABOUT THAT?

IN THE 1960s, A STRANGE THING HAPPENED IN THE WEST.

AS THE BABY BOOMER POST-WAR GENERATION CAME OF AGE, A RECONSTRUCTION OF SOCIETY BEGAN TO TAKE PLACE.

THE YOUNG WERE NOT AS DEFERENTIAL TO AUTHORITY AS THEIR PARENTS WERE.

THE UPPER CLASSES BECAME INCREASINGLY DISCREDITED AS MORAL PARAGONS. ALL HIERARCHIES OF TASTE AND MANNERS WERE LEVELLED.

PEOPLE BEGAN TO DRESS MORE INFORMALLY. THEY ABANDONED HATS, GLOVES, TIES, AND DRESSES. FIRST NAMES BEGAN TO BE USED IN FAVOUR OF TITLES SUCH AS MR, MRS, AND MISS. LEVELS OF TRUST PLUMMETED IN EVERY SOCIAL INSTITUTION.

AS FAITH IN AUTHORITY DECLINED, A WAVE OF ANTI-ESTABLISHMENT FEELING WAS RELEASED. POPULAR MOVEMENTS TO ADDRESS THE OPPRESSION OF MINORITIES BEGAN.

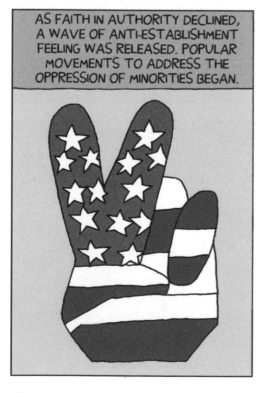

CRITICS ALSO FOCUSED ON ISSUES SUCH AS THE DESPOLIATION OF THE ENVIRONMENT, THE THREAT OF NUCLEAR HOLOCAUST, AND THE VIETNAM WAR.

THE TRADITIONAL IDEAL OF THE FAMILY NOT ONLY BEGAN TO LOOK OLD-FASHIONED, BUT BECAME THE SUBJECT OF RIDICULE.

YOUNG PEOPLE TURNED AWAY FROM WHAT SEEMED TO THEM TO BE A SOULLESS, PLASTIC, MATERIALISTIC LIFESTYLE.

SPONTANEITY, SELF-EXPRESSION, AND THE LOOSENING OF INHIBITIONS BECAME THE NEW VIRTUES...

ALL QUALITIES THAT ARE LIBERAL IN NATURE AND ANATHEMA TO THOSE ON THE RIGHT.

GET A JOB. TAKE A BATH.

MUCH GOOD CAME OUT OF THE 1960s COUNTERCULTURE: EQUAL RIGHTS FOR BLACK PEOPLE, WOMEN, AND GAYS...

RIGHT ON!

AND THE END OF AUTOMATIC DEFERENCE TO THOSE IN A HIGHER SOCIAL POSITION.

THE EMPEROR HAS NO CLOTHES.

BUT ALONG WITH THESE POSITIVE OUTCOMES CAME SOMETHING DARKER.

IN THIS NEW WORLD, MANY OF THE SOCIAL RESTRAINTS THAT SHAPED BEHAVIOUR WERE WEAKENED.

I NEED TO FIND A BIN FOR THIS RUBBISH.

JUST THROW IT ON THE GROUND.

A COMBINATION OF DRUG USE, INDIVIDUALISM, AND LESS PERSONAL SELF-CONTROL HAD UNFORESEEN CONSEQUENCES.

SOMEONE'S BEING ATTACKED DOWN THERE!

NOTHING TO DO WITH US.

A RISING CRIME RATE BEGAN THAT WOULD NOT WANE UNTIL THE 1990s.

I'D GIVE YOU THE NEW CRIME STATS, BUT THEY'VE BEEN STOLEN.

IN BOTH THE US AND EUROPE THE MURDER RATE ROSE TO LEVELS NOT SEEN FOR A CENTURY.

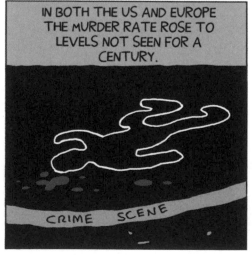

CRIME SCENE

EVERY OTHER TYPE OF MAJOR CRIME ALSO ROCKETED: RAPE, ASSAULT, ROBBERY, AND THEFT.

CITIES BECAME PARTICULARLY DANGEROUS, ESPECIALLY NEW YORK, WHERE THE PARKS AND TRANSIT SYSTEMS BECAME A MUGGERS' PARADISE.

POPULAR CULTURE OF THE 1970s REFLECTED THE RISE IN URBAN CRIME...

IN FILMS SUCH AS 'DIRTY HARRY', 'TAXI DRIVER', AND 'DEATH WISH'.

YOU'RE VERY QUICK TO BLAME THE COUNTERCULTURE FOR ALL THIS MAYHEM...

BUT WASN'T THE CRIME WAVE MORE LIKELY TO HAVE BEEN GENERATED BY THE BOOMING POPULATION OF TEENAGERS AND TWENTY-SOMETHINGS IN THIS ERA?

YOUNG MEN COMMIT THE MAJORITY OF ALL CRIME. IT SEEMS LOGICAL TO SUPPOSE THAT HIGHER NUMBERS OF YOUNG MEN WOULD LEAD TO MORE CRIME, RATHER THAN THE CAUSE BEING CULTURAL. RIGHT?

WRONG! THE NUMBERS JUST DON'T ADD UP. THE NUMBER OF YOUNG PEOPLE IN THE POPULATION ROSE BY 13 PER CENT...

YET THE CRIME RATE WENT UP BY AS MUCH AS 135 PER CENT. QUITE A DISPARITY.

THE FAG-END OF THE PEACE-LOVING 1960s WAS BITTER INDEED.

KAFF! KAFF!

AT THE MARGINS OF SOCIETY SOME DISTURBING CRIMES WERE BEING COMMITTED.

THE 1969 MURDERS OF SEVEN PEOPLE BY THE CULT-LIKE MANSON FAMILY IN CALIFORNIA...

AND THE TRAIL OF DEATH LEFT ACROSS GERMANY BY THE MARXIST TERROR GROUP THE BAADER-MEINHOF GANG (THE RED ARMY FACTION).

THE CRIME BOOM CONTINUED FOR TWENTY YEARS UNTIL IT FINALLY BEGAN TO FADE IN THE 1990s.

SINCE THEN, THE LEVELS OF ALL MAJOR CRIMES ACROSS THE US, CANADA, AND EUROPE HAVE FALLEN DRAMATICALLY.

SO WHAT CAUSED THIS CHANGE? WAS IT ALL DOWN TO MORE EFFICIENT POLICING?

WHAT HAPPENED TO THE MUGGERS?

THEY WERE ARRESTED.

LEVELS OF IMPRISONMENT IN THE US REMAINED FLAT FROM THE 1920s UNTIL THE EARLY 1960s, EVEN DECLINING A LITTLE IN THE 1970s.

SIGH!

BUT THEN RATES SHOT UP ALMOST FIVE-FOLD. MORE THAN TWO MILLION PEOPLE ARE NOW IN AMERICAN PRISONS.

QUIT SHOVING!

THE US HAS THE HIGHEST PRISON POPULATION IN THE WORLD...

THE MAJORITY OF WHOM ARE AFRICAN-AMERICAN MALES FROM DEPRIVED BACKGROUNDS.

MASS INCARCERATION CLEARLY WORKS, NOT JUST AS A WAY OF SKIMMING THE MOST VIOLENT OFF THE STREETS...

BUT AS A DETERRENT TOO.

WELL, NOT SO FAST. CANADA AND WESTERN EUROPE ALSO SAW A DECLINE IN CRIME AND THEY DID NOT BULK UP THEIR PRISON SYSTEM ANYTHING LIKE AS MUCH.

WHAT ABOUT THE THEORY POPULARISED IN THE BOOK 'FREAKONOMICS': THAT RATES OF VIOLENCE HAVE FALLEN IN THE US BECAUSE ABORTION WAS LEGALISED BY THE 1973 ROE VS WADE SUPREME COURT DECISION?

FREAKO NOMICS

ACCORDING TO THIS THEORY, THE UNWANTED CHILDREN WHO WOULD OTHERWISE HAVE GROWN UP TO BE CRIMINALS WERE NOT BORN IN THE FIRST PLACE, BECAUSE THEIR MOTHERS HAD ABORTED THEM INSTEAD.

ANY THEORY THAT ATTEMPTS TO EXPLAIN MASSIVE SOCIAL CHANGE BY ONE EVENT WILL ALMOST CERTAINLY BE WRONG.

IT'S MORE LIKELY THAT WOMEN LIVING IN CRIME-RIDDEN AREAS HAVE MORE UNWANTED CHILDREN...

THAN THAT UNWANTEDNESS ITSELF CAUSES CRIMINAL BEHAVIOUR.

IF ABORTION CREATED LESS CRIME IN SOCIETY, THEN THE DECLINE IN THAT CRIME SHOULD HAVE BEGUN WITH THE YOUNGEST FIRST...

BUT THAT DIDN'T HAPPEN. CRIME REDUCTION BEGAN WITH THE OLDER GENERATION AND THEN WORKED ITS WAY DOWN THE AGE GROUPS.

THIS MAKES PERFECT SENSE, BECAUSE AS PEOPLE AGE THEY GET LESS VIOLENT.

I SEE!

THE FALL IN CRIME CAN BE ATTRIBUTED TO A NUMBER OF COMPLEX CAUSES.

PAH!

NOT JUST HIGHER INCARCERATION RATES, BUT AN INTOLERANCE OF LOW-LEVEL CRIME, SUCH AS VANDALISM AND LITTERING...

PICK THAT UP!

AND A TARGETING OF RAPES, HATE CRIMES, GAY-BASHING, AND CHILD ABUSE.

BLOODY QUEERS!

NONE OF WHICH WAS TAKEN SERIOUSLY BEFORE THE PROGRESSIVE 1960s.

THE DECLINING CRIME RATE CAN ALSO BE ATTRIBUTED TO SOMETHING FAR MORE SUBTLE: A GRADUAL RETURN TO THE VALUES OF PERSONAL RESPONSIBILITY, FAMILY LIFE, AND SELF-CONTROL...

WE'RE BACK.

ALL VALUES USUALLY ASSOCIATED WITH THE RIGHT, RATHER THAN THE LEFT.

HEH!

FROM THE 1980s ONWARDS, WHEN RONALD REAGAN CAME TO POWER IN THE US AND MARGARET THATCHER BECAME PRIME MINISTER IN THE UK, THE POLITICAL DIAL STARTED MOVING TO THE RIGHT. THE ECONOMIC AND HUMANITARIAN DISASTER THAT WAS COMMUNISM COLLAPSED. THIS TOOK THE ROMANCE OUT OF THE EXTREME LEFT'S REVOLUTIONARY ZEAL. CAPITALISM HAD WON, AND A NEW CORPORATE GOLDEN AGE BEGAN.

WE NOW LIVE IN A TIME WHEN THE POLITICAL LEFT HAS ALL BUT DISAPPEARED. THE NEW CENTRE GROUND OF POLITICS IS ON THE RIGHT. IN THE UK THE LABOUR PARTY HAS GRADUALLY DISTANCED ITSELF FROM ITS WORKING CLASS ROOTS TO BECOME A NEOLIBERAL PARTY, WITH MIDDLE CLASS AND MIDDLE ENGLAND VALUES ONLY FRACTIONALLY DIFFERENT FROM THOSE OF ITS OPPONENTS.

IN THE US, THE DEMOCRATIC PARTY HAS MOVED TO THE CENTRE RIGHT TO FILL THE VOID CREATED BY THE REPUBLICANS. WHO HAVE GONE SO FAR TO THE RIGHT THAT THEY HAVE DISINTEGRATED INTO COMPETING EXTREMIST FACTIONS.

I WANT MY COUNTRY BACK!

TAXED ENOUGH ALREADY

DON'T FUND AMACARE

THEY HAVE BECOME A STRANGE MIXTURE OF INTOLERANT RELIGIOUS BELIEFS AND BLIND DEVOTION TO FREE MARKET ECONOMICS.

WE BELIEVE IN GOD, GUNS, AND CAPITALISM.

IN 1970, PRESIDENT RICHARD NIXON SIGNED INTO LAW THE ENVIRONMENTAL PROTECTION AGENCY, CREATED FOR THE PURPOSE OF PROTECTING HUMAN HEALTH AND THE ENVIRONMENT. IT'S IMPOSSIBLE TO IMAGINE A REPUBLICAN PRESIDENT WANTING TO CONSERVE THE ENVIRONMENT IN THE MODERN ERA.

NO REPUBLICAN CANDIDATE TODAY WHO HELD SUCH VIEWS AND WANTED TO RUN FOR THE PRESIDENCY WOULD EVEN BE NOMINATED BY THE PARTY. HE OR SHE WOULD BE SEEN AS UNAMERICAN AND ANTI-BUSINESS.

I AM NOT A CROOK.

FOR LIBERTARIAN REPUBLICANS, THE POWER THE RELIGIOUS RIGHT HOLDS WITHIN THE PARTY IS A PARTICULAR PROBLEM.

US CONGRESSMAN PAUL RYAN WAS MITT ROMNEY'S RUNNING MATE IN THE LATTER'S FAILED BID FOR THE PRESIDENCY IN 2012.

RYAN, WHO MAJORED IN ECONOMICS AND POLITICAL SCIENCE, WAS HUGELY INFLUENCED IN HIS YOUTH BY RIGHT-WING THINKERS SUCH AS FRIEDRICH HAYEK, LUDWIG VON MISES, MILTON FRIEDMAN, AND AYN RAND.

I GREW UP READING AYN RAND AND IT TAUGHT ME QUITE A BIT ABOUT WHO I AM AND WHAT MY VALUE SYSTEMS ARE. IT'S INSPIRED ME SO MUCH THAT IT IS REQUIRED READING IN MY OFFICE FOR ALL MY INTERNS AND MY STAFF.

ATLAS SOCIETY, 2005.

THE FIGHT WE ARE IN HERE, MAKE NO MISTAKE ABOUT IT, IS A FIGHT FOR INDIVIDUALISM VERSUS COLLECTIVISM.

SINCE RAND'S ATHEISM IS ANATHEMA TO THE MAJORITY OF REPUBLICANS, RYAN HAS SINCE HAD TO DISTANCE HIMSELF FROM THE WRITER, CLAIMING THE CONNECTION HAD BEEN EXAGGERATED.

YOU KNOW YOU'VE ARRIVED IN POLITICS WHEN YOU HAVE AN URBAN LEGEND ABOUT YOU. THIS ONE IS MINE.

A CURIOUS THING TO SAY WHEN HIS SPEECH FOR THE ATLAS SOCIETY WAS RECORDED FOR ALL TO HEAR.

CLAP! CLAP! CLAP! CLAP! CLAP!

AS CHAIRMAN OF THE UNITED STATES HOUSE OF REPRESENTATIVES' BUDGET COMMITTEE SINCE 2011...

RYAN HAS PRESENTED A SERIES OF BUDGET PLANS DESIGNED TO APPEAL TO HARDCORE REPUBLICAN VALUES.

THESE PROPOSALS WOULD HAVE INCREASED MILITARY SPENDING AND GIVEN LARGE TAX CUTS TO THE RICH...

AWESOME!

WHILE DELIVERING THE INEVITABLE HUGE CUTS TO SOCIAL PROGRAMMES IN AN ATTEMPT TO FOOT THE BILL.

HELP!

RYAN'S PLANS, NEVER TAKEN UP BY THE SENATE, HAVE NEVERTHELESS PLEASED THE VAST MAJORITY WITHIN THE CONSERVATIVE MOVEMENT.

THAT'S RIGHT!

WHETHER RELIGIOUS OR NOT, TAX CUTS AND THE DISMANTLING OF WELFARE ARE SUBJECTS THOSE ON THE RIGHT CAN ALWAYS UNITE ON...

WE'RE DONE WITH SUPPORTING DEADBEATS ON WELFARE.

THE EXCEPTION TO THIS BEING MODERATE REPUBLICANS, WHO ARE AN ENDANGERED SPECIES IN MODERN AMERICA ANYWAY.

THOSE PEOPLE ARE TRAITORS.

MODERATES HAVE BEEN INCREASINGLY MARGINALISED AS THE PARTY HAS MOVED TO A POSITION COMPATIBLE WITH AYN RAND'S VIEWS.

A MAJOR FACTOR IN THIS LURCH TO THE EXTREME RIGHT IS THE RISE OF THE TEA PARTY.

MORE TEA, SENATOR?

THE NAME 'TEA PARTY' IS A REFERENCE TO THE BOSTON TEA PARTY, A PROTEST BY COLONISTS IN 1773 WHO OBJECTED TO A BRITISH TAX ON TEA.

WHY, YES!

THE TEA PARTY IS A LOOSE AFFILIATION OF NATIONAL AND LOCAL GROUPS THAT DETERMINE THEIR OWN PLATFORMS AND AGENDA WITHOUT CENTRAL LEADERSHIP.

I FORMED MY OWN GROUP. ANYONE CAN.

THEY ARE A GRASSROOTS MOVEMENT PROMOTED BY RIGHT-WING MEDIA AND SUPPORTED BY RICH DONORS.

HELLO!

THE BILLIONAIRE BROTHERS DAVID H. KOCH AND CHARLES G. KOCH OF KOCH INDUSTRIES HAVE PROVIDED FINANCIAL SUPPORT...

WE HAVE A BIG PILE OF MONEY FOR YOU.

VIA ORGANISATIONS SUCH AS AMERICANS FOR PROSPERITY, AND CITIZENS FOR A SOUND ECONOMY, WHICH THEY FOUNDED.

WOW!

ALONG WITH MURRAY ROTHBARD, CHARLES KOCH ALSO FOUNDED THE INFLUENTIAL LIBERTARIAN THINK TANK THE CATO INSTUTE.

THAT'S CORRECT!

KOCH INDUSTRIES HAS AN ANNUAL REVENUE ESTIMATED TO BE A HUNDRED MILLION DOLLARS.

THE KOCHS OPERATE OIL REFINERIES IN ALASKA, TEXAS, AND MINNESOTA, AND CONTROL FOUR THOUSAND MILES OF PIPELINE.

THEY'RE GOOD AMERICANS.

THEIR COMBINED FORTUNE OF THIRTY-FIVE BILLION DOLLARS IS EXCEEDED ONLY BY WARREN BUFFETT'S AND BILL GATES'.

THERE'S NOTHING WRONG WITH BEING RICH.

THE BROTHERS BELIEVE IN LOW PERSONAL AND CORPORATE TAXES, MINIMAL SOCIAL SERVICES FOR THE NEEDY, AND MUCH LESS OVERSIGHT OF INDUSTRY.

IT'S NOT LIKE THEY'RE EXPLOITING PEOPLE.

THE ABOLITION OF THE NIXON-CREATED ENVIRONMENTAL PROTECTION AGENCY IS A MAJOR OBJECTIVE.

THE KOCHS DID NOT START THE TEA PARTY. MANY ELEMENTS CAME TOGETHER TO CREATE THE MOVEMENT.

BUT THE ELECTION OF BARACK OBAMA TO THE WHITE HOUSE AND THE 2008 FINANCIAL CRISIS PROVIDED THE CATALYST.

THUD!

ON FEBRUARY 19, 2009, IN A BROADCAST AT THE CHICAGO MERCANTILE EXCHANGE, THE CNBC BUSINESS NEWS NETWORK EDITOR RICK SANTELLI, A SELF-STYLED RANDIAN...

CRITICISED THE GOVERNMENT PLAN TO REFINANCE THE MORTGAGES OF HOMEOWNERS WHO HAD LOST OUT DURING THE CRISIS.

THIS WAS THE HOMEOWNER AFFORDABILITY AND STABILITY PLAN, ANNOUNCED TWO DAYS PREVIOUSLY.

SANTELLI WAS FURIOUS THAT THE GOVERNMENT WAS SUBSIDISING 'LOSERS' MORTGAGES' WITH TAXPAYERS' MONEY.

HOW MANY OF YOU PEOPLE WANNA PAY FOR YOUR NEIGHBOUR'S MORTGAGE?

TO CHEERS FROM THE TRADERS AROUND HIM, SANTELLI SUGGESTED THEY SHOULD HAVE A TEA PARTY IN JULY.

YOU KNOW, CUBA USED TO HAVE MANSIONS AND A RELATIVELY DECENT ECONOMY. THEY MOVED FROM THE INDIVIDUAL TO THE COLLECTIVE. NOW THEY'RE DRIVING '54 CHEVYS.

NOTE THE RANDIAN TERMINOLOGY HERE.

ALL YOU CAPITALISTS THAT WANT TO SHOW UP TO LAKE MICHIGAN, I'M GOING TO START ORGANISING. WE'RE GOING TO BE DUMPING IN SOME DERIVATIVE SECURITIES. WHAT DO YOU THINK ABOUT THAT?

IN HIS ANGER, SANTELLI HAD CONVENIENTLY FORGOTTEN THAT IT WAS THE GOVERNMENT'S NONEXISTENT REGULATION OF THE DERIVATIVES MARKET...

ALONG WITH THE GREED OF BANKERS AND THOSE IN THE MORTGAGE INDUSTRY, NOT GOVERNMENT INTERVENTION...

THAT HAD CAUSED THE CATASTROPHE IN THE FIRST PLACE.

THE NEXT DAY AROUND FIFTY CONSERVATIVE ACTIVISTS TOOK PART IN A CONFERENCE CALL THAT GAVE BIRTH TO THE TEA PARTY MOVEMENT.

WEBSITES SUCH AS TEAPARTY.COM WERE LIVE WITHIN TWELVE HOURS OF SANTELLI'S BROADCAST.

ANOTHER SITE, RETEAPARTY.COM, WAS RECEIVING 11,000 VISITORS A DAY WITHIN TWO WEEKS OF ITS LAUNCH.

THE EMERGENCE OF THE TEA PARTY MOVEMENT WAS AMPLIFIED BY RIGHT-WING MEDIA OUTLETS, SUCH AS FOX NEWS, AND TALK RADIO HOSTS, LIKE RUSH LIMBAUGH AND BILL O'REILLY.

PROTESTS BEGAN ALL ACROSS THE COUNTRY, OPPOSING HIGH TAXES, BIG GOVERNMENT, AND POLITICAL CORRECTNESS. SIGNS REFERENCING AYN RAND STARTED TO APPEAR AT THESE GATHERINGS.

AYN RAND WAS RIGHT!

WE RESENT THAT HALF THE PEOPLE PAY ALL THE TAXES WHILE THE OTHER HALF PAY NONE.

WHO IS JOHN GALT?

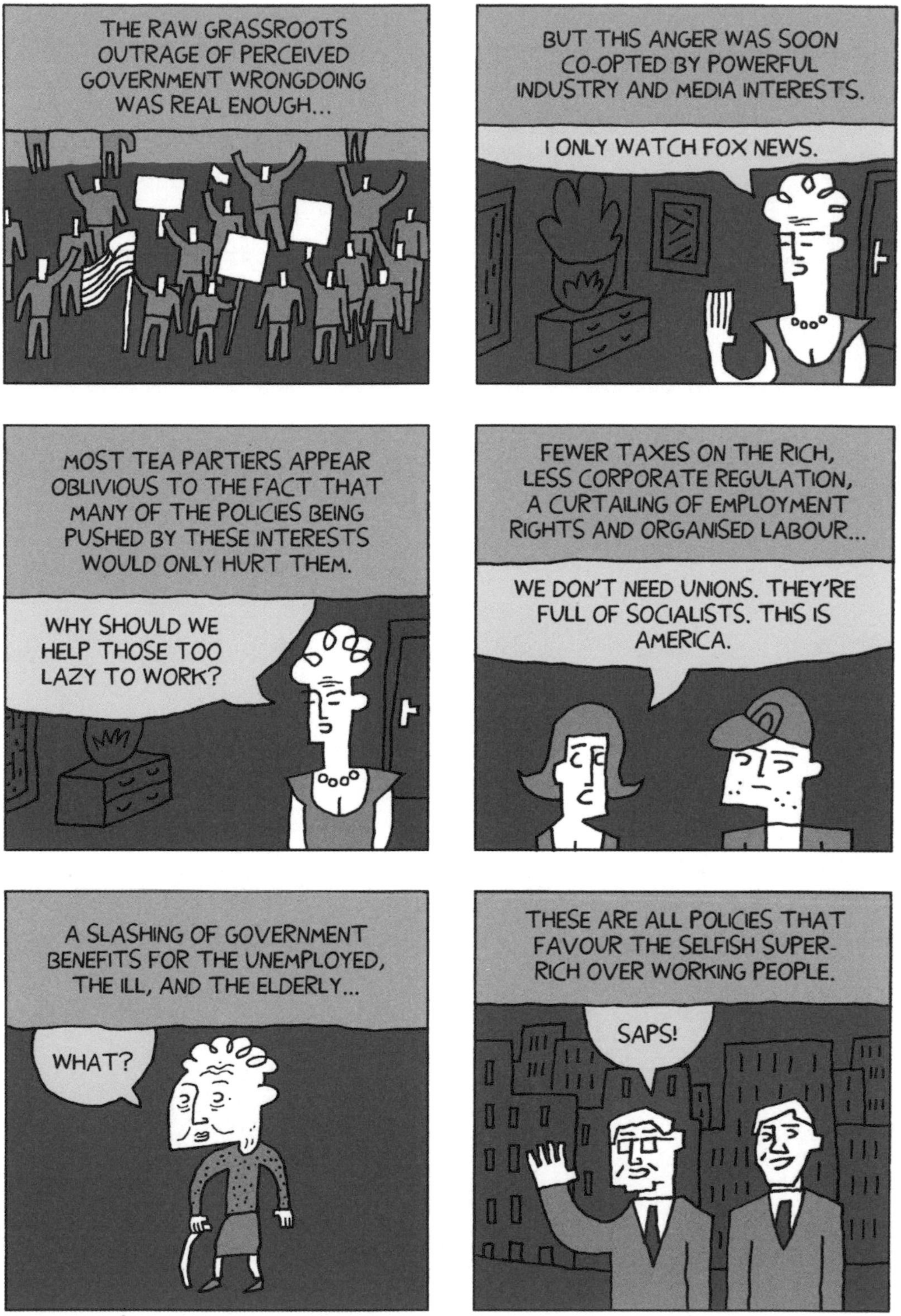
THE RAW GRASSROOTS OUTRAGE OF PERCEIVED GOVERNMENT WRONGDOING WAS REAL ENOUGH...
BUT THIS ANGER WAS SOON CO-OPTED BY POWERFUL INDUSTRY AND MEDIA INTERESTS.
I ONLY WATCH FOX NEWS.
MOST TEA PARTIERS APPEAR OBLIVIOUS TO THE FACT THAT MANY OF THE POLICIES BEING PUSHED BY THESE INTERESTS WOULD ONLY HURT THEM.
WHY SHOULD WE HELP THOSE TOO LAZY TO WORK?
FEWER TAXES ON THE RICH, LESS CORPORATE REGULATION, A CURTAILING OF EMPLOYMENT RIGHTS AND ORGANISED LABOUR...
WE DON'T NEED UNIONS. THEY'RE FULL OF SOCIALISTS. THIS IS AMERICA.
A SLASHING OF GOVERNMENT BENEFITS FOR THE UNEMPLOYED, THE ILL, AND THE ELDERLY...
WHAT?
THESE ARE ALL POLICIES THAT FAVOUR THE SELFISH SUPER-RICH OVER WORKING PEOPLE.
SAPS!

IN THIS WAY CORPORATE AMERICA HAS COERCED TEA PARTIERS TO ACT AGAINST THEIR OWN INTERESTS...

BY HAVING THEM VOTE INTO OFFICE POLITICIANS WHO OPENLY FAVOUR BIG BUSINESS AND WALL STREET...

OVER THE PEOPLE IN THEIR OWN COMMUNITIES WHO HAVE LOST JOBS AND HOMES.

I'M LIVING IN MY CAR.

THERE IS A STRONG CURRENT OF RACISM RUNNING THROUGH THE TEA PARTY.

OBAMA-NOMICS MONKEY SEE... MONKEY SPEND!

THEY HATE WELFARE BECAUSE THEY FEAR TAX PAYERS' MONEY IS BEING GIVEN TO MINORITIES.

SAVE WHITE AMERICA

ACTUAL TEA PARTY SIGNS.

THEY ARE OBSESSED WITH MUSLIMS AND ISLAM.

A MOSQUE IS JUST A TERRORIST CENTRE.

THEY'RE DEEPLY WORRIED ABOUT UNDOCUMENTED IMMIGRANTS, ESPECIALLY THOSE COMING FROM MEXICO.

THEY ESPECIALLY HATE PRESIDENT OBAMA.

THERE ARE PARALLELS TO THE TEA PARTY MOVEMENT IN OTHER COUNTRIES...

SUCH AS THE UNITED KINGDOM INDEPENDENCE PARTY IN THE UK.

UKIP IS A RIGHT-WING, POPULIST, ANTI-IMMIGRATION AND ANTI-EUROPEAN UNION PARTY.

THEY HOLD TWENTY-FOUR OF THE UK's SEVENTY-THREE SEATS IN THE EUROPEAN PARLIAMENT.

UKIP DID WELL IN THE 2008 LOCAL ELECTIONS, COMING FOURTH IN THE NUMBER OF COUNCIL SEATS WON AND THIRD IN THE NATIONAL SHARE OF THE VOTE. IN 2014 THEY GAINED 163 LOCAL SEATS. DESPITE THIS SURGE, THEY HAVE YET TO GAIN A SINGLE SEAT IN THE UK PARLIAMENT.

NIGEL FARAGE, UKIP LEADER.

IT IS A PARTY DEFINED ENTIRELY BY ITS PREJUDICES. BARELY A WEEK GOES BY WHEN ONE OF THEIR NUMBER DOESN'T SAY SOMETHING BIZARRE, INSULTING, OR OUTLANDISH.

A UKIP MEMBER OF THE EUROPEAN PARLIAMENT ASKED WHY BRITAIN WAS GIVING AID TO 'BONGO BONGO LAND'.

A UKIP COUNCILLOR TODAY CLAIMED IT WAS GOD'S ANGER AT GAY MARRIAGE THAT HAD CAUSED THE RECENT WIDESPREAD FLOODING.

MUCH CONSERVATIVE PREJUDICE STEMS FROM A SENSE OF UNFAIRNESS WHEN THEY SEE OTHERS GETTING SOMETHING THEY DID NOT EARN. ON THE LEFT, FAIRNESS MEANS EQUALITY, BUT ON THE RIGHT IT MEANS PROPORTIONALITY...

WHICH IN THIS CASE MEANS THAT PEOPLE SHOULD ONLY BE REWARDED IN PROPORTION TO THEIR CONTRIBUTIONS, EVEN IF THIS GUARANTEES UNEQUAL OUTCOMES.

IT IS CERTAINLY WRONG FOR ANYONE TO LIVE AT THE EXPENSE OF ANOTHER. UNFORTUNATELY, RIGHT-WING POLITICS OFTEN FAILS TO MAKE ANY DISTINCTION BETWEEN FREELOADERS AND THE POOR.

THE UNEMPLOYED ARE TREATED WITH SUSPICION, WHILE WORKING PEOPLE ARE INCREASINGLY DENIED A DECENT LEVEL OF EARNINGS.

I WORK FULL-TIME, YET CANNOT PAY MY MORTGAGE. WHERE'S THE PROPORTIONALITY IN THAT?

WHAT MOTIVATES CONSERVATIVES IS THE NEED TO PROTECT THE STATUS QUO, OR, EVEN BETTER, TURN THE CLOCK BACK TO SOME NOSTALGIC AND OFTEN IMAGINARY GOLDEN AGE. THE CONSERVATIVE MOVEMENT IS NOT FILLED WITH UNCARING SOCIOPATHS. THEY HAVE A STRONG SENSE OF MORALITY.

THERE IS NOTHING WRONG IN A BELIEF IN LAWS, FAMILY LIFE, CUSTOMS, INSTITUTIONS, TRADITIONS, NATIONS, AND RELIGIONS. LIBERALS TEND TO UNDERESTIMATE THE IMPORTANCE OF SUCH STRUCTURES IN THE CREATION OF A STABLE AND COHESIVE SOCIETY. CONSERVATIVES DO CARE, BUT THEY FIND IT HARD TO EXTEND THAT CARE TO THOSE OUTSIDE THEIR OWN GROUP.

MUCH LIKE THE TEA PARTY, UKIP's POPULARITY IS A VOTER RESPONSE TO THE INDIFFERENCE OF THE MAINSTREAM POLITICAL CLASS WHO HAVE OFFERED NO SOLUTION TO FALLING WAGES, RISING HOUSING COSTS, AND UNEMPLOYMENT.

INSTEAD OF ADDRESSING THESE PROBLEMS, UKIP HAS PLACED THE BLAME SQUARELY ON IMMIGRATION, MIGRANT WORKERS, AND THE UNITED KINGDOM'S MEMBERSHIP OF THE EUROPEAN UNION.

ROMANIANS ARE TAKING OUR JOBS.

IN FACT, UKIP GENERALLY SERVES THE SAME VESTED INTERESTS THAT BENEFIT FROM THE CURRENT STATUS QUO. IT IS LARGELY FUNDED BY THE MULTI-MILLIONAIRE PROPERTY DEVELOPER PAUL SYKES.

HOW DO?

NIGEL FARAGE HIMSELF IS HARDLY A MAN OF THE PEOPLE. HE HAS THE PRIVILEGED BACKGROUND OF ANY CAREER POLITICIAN. A PUBLIC-SCHOOL--EDUCATED, EX-CONSERVATIVE PARTY MEMBER WHO USED TO BE A COMMODITY TRADER IN THE CITY OF LONDON.

I WORKED AT THE LONDON METAL EXCHANGE.

NOT SURPRISINGLY, FARAGE THINKS THAT THE 2008 FINANCIAL CRISIS WAS CAUSED BY GOVERNMENT FAILURE ALONE, RATHER THAN BY BANKER GREED.

APART FROM WANTING TO LEAVE THE EU AND BEING AGAINST IMMIGRATION, UKIP FAVOURS THE USUAL ROUND OF RIGHT-WING TAX CUTS AND BENEFIT REDUCTIONS, ALONG WITH AN INCREASE IN DEFENCE SPENDING AND PRISON-BUILDING.

HOW'S THAT GOING TO HELP THE GROWING NUMBER OF POOR?

ALSO IN THE MIX IS AN ATTACK ON EMPLOYMENT RIGHTS. IN ITS LITTLE-PUBLICISED 2013 SMALL BUSINESS MANIFESTO, UKIP PROPOSED ABOLISHING THE RIGHT TO MATERNITY PAY, PAID HOLIDAY, AND SICK PAY.

IT IS USING PREJUDICE AND RACIAL HATRED IN ORDER TO FOOL PEOPLE INTO SCRAPPING THEIR BASIC RIGHTS. IT IS THE BULLYING FACE OF THE ESTABLISHMENT.

WHAT ARE YOU, SOME KIND OF LEFTY?

HERE ARE SOME EXAMPLES OF WHAT THAT MEANS IN PRACTICE. BRITAIN 2013: FOR THE FIRST TIME SINCE THE SECOND WORLD WAR, THE RED CROSS HAD TO GIVE AID IN THE UK, AS WELFARE CUTS, LOW WAGES, AND RISING PRICES CAUSED A DRAMATIC RISE IN THE NUMBER OF FOOD BANKS FOR THE HUNGRY.

WILL YOU HELP ME STACK THESE BOXES?

SURE.

USERS OF THESE FOOD BANKS HAD TO BE REFERRED BY A DOCTOR OR SOCIAL WORKER. THEY WERE TYPICALLY GIVEN THREE DAYS' WORTH OF NON-PERISHABLE FOODS.

A REPORT BY THE AID AGENCY OXFAM AND CHURCH GROUP ACTION ON POVERTY, PUBLISHED IN MAY 2013, STATED THAT HALF A MILLION PEOPLE HAD TURNED TO FOOD BANKS TO FEED THEMSELVES AND THEIR FAMILIES: A NUMBER TRIPLE THAT OF THE PREVIOUS YEAR.

THE NUMBER OF PEOPLE WHO RECEIVED EMERGENCY FOOD.

2007/08	2008/09	2009/10	2010/11	2011/12	2012/13	2013/14
13,849	25,899	40,898	61,468	128,697	346,992	913,138

FIGURES FROM THE TRUSSELL TRUST FOOD BANK PROJECT.

AFTER THE WELFARE REFORM ACTS OF 2007 AND 2012, PEOPLE WITH DISABLITIES IN THE UK BECAME THE SUBJECT OF ASSESSMENTS IN ORDER TO DETERMINE THEIR LEVEL OF ABILITY AND DISABILITY.

I'VE BEEN SUMMONED.

BROUGHT IN INITIALLY BY THE LABOUR GOVERNMENT, THE NEW WORK CAPABILITY ASSESSMENT WAS THEN EXPANDED AND PUSHED AGGRESSIVELY BY THE CONSERVATIVE-LIBERAL DEMOCRAT COALITION WHICH CAME INTO POWER AFTER THE 2008 FINANCIAL CRISIS.

OUTSOURCED BY THE DEPARTMENT FOR WORK AND PENSIONS TO THE FRENCH MULTINATIONAL IT SERVICES AND CONSULTING COMPANY ATOS, THE ASSESSMENT PROCEDURE SOON GAINED A REPUTATION FOR HARSHNESS AND EVEN CRUELTY.

ATOS

ATOS HEALTHCARE USED A COMPUTER-BASED POINTS SYSTEM TO ASSESS CLAIMANTS. A QUESTIONNAIRE WAS READ TO THE INDIVIDUAL AND THEIR RESPONSES WERE NOTED, AFTER WHICH THERE WAS OCCASIONALLY A SHORT EXAM.

DID YOU WALK HERE?

THE GOVERNMENT'S OWN STATISTICS REVEAL THAT, BETWEEN JANUARY 2010 AND JANUARY 2011, 10,600 SICK AND DISABLED PEOPLE DIED WITHIN SIX WEEKS OF THEIR BENEFITS BEING STOPPED.

I'M NOT FEELING WELL AT ALL.

GOVERNMENT FIGURES ALSO REVEALED THAT, OF THOSE WHO HAD BEEN FOUND FIT FOR WORK, 1,300 DIED SHORTLY AFTER THEIR ASSESSMENT BY ATOS.

UGH!

YOU'RE NOT FOOLING ANYONE.

ATOS ASSESSORS HAVE FOUND PATIENTS WITH BRAIN DAMAGE, TERMINAL CANCER, MULTIPLE SCLEROSIS, AND PARKINSON'S DISEASE TO BE FIT FOR WORK.

I'M STILL NOT CONVINCED.

LINDA WOOTTON, A DOUBLE HEART AND LUNG TRANSPLANT PATIENT, DIED ONLY NINE DAYS AFTER ATOS OFFICIALS RULED THAT SHE WAS FIT ENOUGH TO RETURN TO WORK.

OUR SYMPATHY GOES OUT TO MRS WOOTTON'S FAMILY. A DECISION ON WHETHER SOMEONE IS WELL ENOUGH TO RETURN TO WORK IS TAKEN FOLLOWING A THOROUGH ASSESSMENT AND AFTER CONSIDERATION OF ALL SUPPORTING MEDICAL EVIDENCE.

DEPARTMENT FOR WORK AND PENSIONS SPOKESMAN

COLIN TRAYNOR, A TWENTY-NINE-YEAR-OLD MAN DIAGNOSED WITH 'GRAND MAL' EPILEPSY, WAS ASSESSED AS FIT FOR WORK. HE HAD HIS INCAPACITY BENEFIT CUT BY £70 A WEEK, PLACING HIM UNDER ENORMOUS STRESS.

RAY TRAYNOR, COLIN'S FATHER

TRAYNOR'S APPEAL AGAINST THIS DECISION WAS SUCCESSFUL, BUT IT CAME TOO LATE. FIVE WEEKS PREVIOUSLY, A MASSIVE SEIZURE HAD ALREADY KILLED HIM.

I FIRMLY – 100 PER CENT – BELIEVE THAT THE SYSTEM KILLED MY SON.

THERE ARE MANY MORE CASES LIKE THIS. DAVID BARR, TWENTY-EIGHT, WAS ON ANTIDEPRESSANT AND ANTIPSYCHOTIC MEDICATION. HE THREW HIMSELF FROM THE FORTH ROAD BRIDGE AFTER LEARNING THAT THE DECISION TO STOP HIS BENEFITS HAD BEEN UPHELD.

CORRELATION IS, OF COURSE, NOT CAUSATION. AN ATOS ASSESSMENT FOLLOWED BY A DEATH DOES NOT NECESSARILY MEAN THAT THE FIRST EVENT CAUSED THE SECOND.

BUT THE LARGE NUMBERS OF SUCCESSFULLY APPEALED DECISIONS – SOME 37 PER CENT – DOES SUGGEST THAT THE PROCEDURE USED IS OVERLY SIMPLISTIC AND HARSH...

RESULTING IN THE DISTRESS OF MANY THOUSANDS OF THE MOST VULNERABLE IN SOCIETY. HOW THEN CAN THIS NOT BE CAUSING HARM TO THOSE ALREADY SUFFERING LIFE - THREATENING CONDITIONS?

THE GOVERNMENT'S RESPONSE TO CRITICISMS OF THE WORK CAPABILITY ASSESSMENT PROCESS HAS BEEN CALLOUS AND DISHONEST.

IN MARCH 2013, MINISTERS STATED THAT 878,000 PEOPLE WHO WERE ON INCAPACITY BENEFIT DROPPED THEIR CLAIM RATHER THAN UNDERGO THE TEST.

IT LATER EMERGED THAT THIS FIGURE WAS CALCULATED BY ADDING UP THE 20,000 CLAIMANTS EVERY MONTH WHO LEAVE THE BENEFITS SYSTEM WITHOUT UNDERGOING WORK CAPABILITY ASSESSMENT OVER FOUR YEARS...

THESE FIGURES DEMONSTRATE HOW THE WELFARE SYSTEM WAS BROKEN...

GRANT SHAPPS, CONSERVATIVE PARTY CHAIRMAN

WHICH THE DEPARTMENT FOR WORK AND PENSIONS' OWN RESEARCH REVEALS IS LARGELY OWING TO THE FACT THAT MANY WILL SEE AN IMPROVEMENT IN THEIR CONDITIONS, OR WILL RETURN TO WORK WHILE STILL ILL, OR CLAIM A BENEFIT MORE APPROPRIATE FOR THEIR SITUATION.

AND WHY OUR REFORMS ARE SO IMPORTANT.

IN OTHER WORDS, PEOPLE WHO ACHIEVED BETTER HEALTH, PLUS THOSE WHO HAD TAKEN JOBS DESPITE ONGOING ILLNESS, WERE ALL PORTRAYED BY THE GOVERNMENT AS SCROUNGERS.

I BET YOU CAN REALLY SEE.

THIS FOCUS ON ALLEGED FRAUD AND OVERCLAIMING TO JUSTIFY CUTS IN BENEFITS HAS CAUSED AN INCREASE IN RESENTMENT AND ABUSE DIRECTED AT DISABLED PEOPLE.

GET UP AND WALK, YOU LAZY SHIT!

SOME OF THE COUNTRY'S BIGGEST CHARITIES — SCOPE, MENCAP, LEONARD CHESHIRE DISABILITY, THE ROYAL NATIONAL INSTITUTE OF BLIND PEOPLE, AND THE DISABILITY ALLIANCE — ALL WARN OF A RISE IN THE NUMBER OF PEOPLE CONTACTING THEM, SAYING THAT THEY ARE REGULARLY TAUNTED IN THE STREET.

ACCORDING TO THE 'GUARDIAN', THESE CHARITIES ALSO SAID THAT INFLAMMATORY MEDIA COVERAGE PLAYED A ROLE IN THIS, BUT THEY PRIMARILY BLAMED MINISTERS AND CIVIL SERVANTS FOR REPEATEDLY HIGHLIGHTING THE SUPPOSED ABUSE OF DISABILITY BENEFITS.

SCOPE'S REGULAR POLLING OF PEOPLE WITH DISABILITIES SHOWED THAT, IN AUGUST 2013, 81 PER CENT OF DISABLED PEOPLE SAID THAT PUBLIC ATTITUDES HAD NOT IMPROVED IN THE PREVIOUS TWELVE MONTHS — WITH 22 PER CENT SAYING ATTITUDES HAD GOT WORSE.

MY NEW YEAR'S RESOLUTION FOR 2012 WAS TO BECOME DISABLED. NOTHING TOO SERIOUS. MAYBE JUST A BIT OF BAD BACKACHE OR ONE THOSE NEWLY INVENTED ILLNESSES WHICH MAKE YOU A BIT PEAKY — FIBROMYALGIA OR ME.

ROD LIDDLE, JOURNALIST.

I THINK WE SHOULD ALL PRETEND TO BE DISABLED FOR A MONTH OR SO, CLAIM BENEFITS, AND HOPE THE GOVERNMENT SORTS OUT THIS MESS.

SUCH COMMENTS BY JOURNALISTS ONLY ENCOURAGE THE BELIEF THAT DISABILITY BENEFIT FRAUD IS WIDESPREAD, BUT THE GOVERNMENT'S OWN FIGURES SHOW THAT THE ESTIMATED OVERPAYMENT OF DISABILITY LIVING ALLOWANCE DUE TO FRAUD MAKES UP ONLY 0.5 PER CENT OF TOTAL SPENDING.

WE HAVE LOT OF OF WORK TO DO TODAY.

BY COMPARISON, OVERPAYMENTS CAUSED BY OFFICIAL ERRORS ARE HIGHER AT 0.8 PER CENT, YET, DESPITE THE ACTUAL FACTS, THE REMORSELESS DELUGE OF NEGATIVE PROPAGANDA AGAINST DISABILITY CLAIMANTS HAS SUCCESSFULLY HARDENED THE BRITISH PUBLIC'S HEARTS AGAINST THOSE ON BENEFITS.

SO WHAT'S NEXT?

THERE IS A GENERAL BELIEF THAT THE MAJORITY OF THE WELFARE BUDGET GOES ON UNEMPLOYMENT AND INCAPACITY BENEFITS. IN FACT, MOST WELFARE SPENDING GOES ON STATE PENSIONS AND SUPPORT FOR THOSE IN WORK BUT ON LOW INCOMES. JOBSEEKER'S ALLOWANCE IS ONE OF THE SMALLEST BENEFITS, AT LESS THAN THREE PER CENT OF THE ENTIRE WELFARE BILL.

SOURCE: INSTITUTE OF FISCAL STUDIES.

| ELDERLY 42.3% | SICK AND DISABLED 15.5% | WIDOWS 0.3% | UNEMPLOYED 2.6% |
| FAMILIES 18.4% | LOW INCOME 20.8% | OTHERS 0.1% | |

THE DEPARTMENT FOR WORK AND PENSIONS, WHICH IS RESPONSIBLE FOR PAYMENT OF STATE PENSIONS, HOUSING BENEFIT, AND UNEMPLOYMENT BENEFIT, SAYS THAT FRAUD COSTS IT £1.2 BILLION. THE INLAND REVENUE, WHICH PAYS OUT CHILD BENEFIT AND WORKING TAX CREDITS, IDENTIFIED A FURTHER £870 MILLION. ADD THIS TOGETHER AND YOU GET A FIGURE OF AROUND £2 BILLION.

FIGURES FOR THE YEAR 2011/12

TOTAL ANNUAL BENEFITS	UNCLAIMED BENEFITS	BENEFIT ERROR	BENEFIT FRAUD
£194.3 BILLION	£12.3 BILLION	£3.4 BILLION	£2.0 BILLION

£2 BILLION IS A LARGE FIGURE, EVEN IF IT IS DWARFED BY BENEFIT ERRORS AND UNCLAIMED BENEFITS, AND IT IS ONLY RIGHT THAT IT SHOULD BE TACKLED. HOWEVER, WHEN YOU LOOK AT THE COLOSSAL AMOUNT OF MONEY LOST TO THE TREASURY BY TAX AVOIDANCE SCHEMES AND OUTRIGHT TAX FRAUD, YOU HAVE TO WONDER WHY A GOVERNMENT WOULD MAKE SUCH A HUGE EFFORT TO DEAL WITH THE SMALLER PROBLEM, WHILE DOING ALMOST NOTHING TO DEAL WITH THE LARGER ONE?

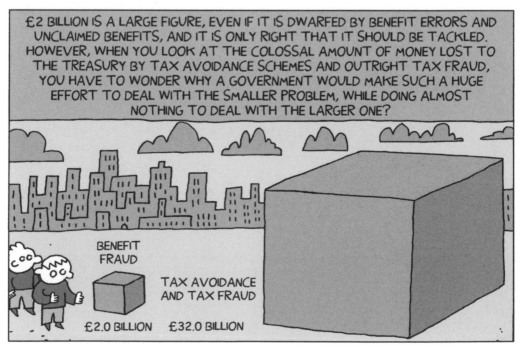

BENEFIT FRAUD

TAX AVOIDANCE AND TAX FRAUD

£2.0 BILLION   £32.0 BILLION

BY COMPARISON WITH BENEFIT FRAUD, TAX AVOIDANCE IS HARDLY MENTIONED BY GOVERNMENT MINISTERS.

IT'S ALMOST AS IF THE GOVERNMENT HAD NO INTEREST IN COLLECTING TAXES.

IN MAY 2012, THERE WAS A RESOLUTION IN THE EUROPEAN PARLIAMENT, CALLING FOR MEASURES TO COMBAT TAX FRAUD AND TAX AVOIDANCE WITHIN THE EUROPEAN UNION. IT CALLED FOR THE INTRODUCTION OF AUTOMATIC DATA-SHARING TO CRACK DOWN ON THOSE SEEKING TO HIDE THEIR MONEY FROM THE AUTHORITIES. IT ALSO DEMANDED THAT CROSS-BORDER COMPANIES FROM ALL SECTORS REPORT ON THEIR PAYMENTS TO GOVERNMENT, IN ORDER BETTER TO DETECT CORPORATE TAX AVOIDANCE.

THE RESOLUTION WAS BACKED BY ALL THE MAJOR EUROPEAN GROUPS INCLUDING THE SOCIALISTS AND DEMOCRATS, THE EUROPEAN PEOPLE'S PARTY, THE ALLIANCE OF LIBERALS AND DEMOCRATS FOR EUROPE, AND THE GREENS...

BUT NOT BY THE BRITISH CONSERVATIVES, WHO VOTED AGAINST THE MEASURES, ALONG WITH THE UNITED KINGDOM INDEPENDENCE PARTY (UKIP).

FIGURES PUBLISHED BY THE CHARITY ACTION AID IN 2013 SHOWED THAT, OF THE TOP 100 COMPANIES LISTED ON THE UK FINANCIAL TIMES SHARE INDEX, ONLY TWO DID NOT USE TAX HAVENS AS A TACTIC TO AVOID PAYING CORPORATION TAX.

THESE COMPANIES INCLUDED STARBUCKS, AMAZON, GOOGLE, VODAFONE, AND APPLE. ALSO ON THE LIST WERE BANKS SUCH AS BARCLAYS, HSBC, THE ROYAL BANK OF SCOTLAND, AND LLOYDS.

IF I BOYCOTTED ALL THESE TAX-AVOIDING FIRMS, I WOULDN'T BE ABLE TO SHOP, BANK, OR USE THE INTERNET.

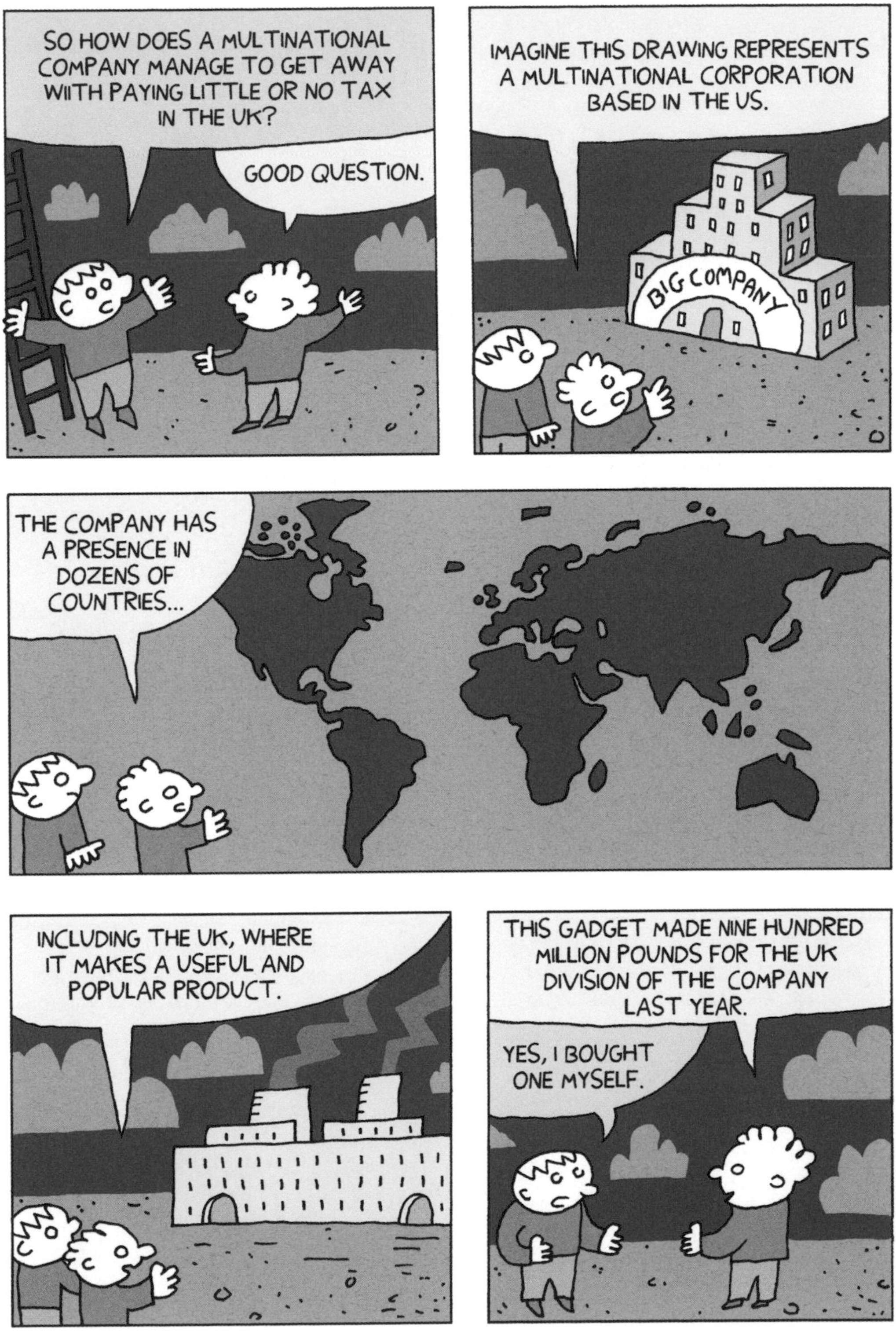
SO HOW DOES A MULTINATIONAL COMPANY MANAGE TO GET AWAY WIITH PAYING LITTLE OR NO TAX IN THE UK?
GOOD QUESTION.
IMAGINE THIS DRAWING REPRESENTS A MULTINATIONAL CORPORATION BASED IN THE US.
BIG COMPANY
THE COMPANY HAS A PRESENCE IN DOZENS OF COUNTRIES...
INCLUDING THE UK, WHERE IT MAKES A USEFUL AND POPULAR PRODUCT.
THIS GADGET MADE NINE HUNDRED MILLION POUNDS FOR THE UK DIVISION OF THE COMPANY LAST YEAR.
YES, I BOUGHT ONE MYSELF.

HOWEVER, CORPORATION TAX ISN'T PAID ON SALES, BUT ON PROFITS, AND SOMEHOW THE UK ARM OF THIS COMPANY ONLY MADE A PROFIT OF TEN MILLION THAT YEAR.

WHAT?

YES, THAT'S RIGHT! YOU SEE, THE UK DIVISION SPENT A LOT OF MONEY IMPORTING PARTS FROM THE COMPANY'S HONG KONG FACTORY.

THEN, ONCE THE PRODUCT WAS MADE, IT WAS SOLD ON CHEAPLY TO THE COMPANY'S DIVISION IN IRELAND...

WHICH THEN SOLD THE ITEMS ACROSS EUROPE, MAKING MANY MILLIONS.

THE RESULT WAS THAT THE COMPANY MADE MOST OF ITS PROFITS IN LOW-TAX IRELAND AND HONG KONG...

UK
23%

HONG KONG
17%

IRELAND
12%

AND IT DOESN'T EVEN PAY TAX ON THE IRISH SALES, AS THAT DIVISION IS RUN FROM NEW YORK.

YOU SEE, THE US TREATS THE COMPANY AS IRISH, BECAUSE ALL ITS BUSINESS IS DONE OVERSEAS.

NOTHING TO DO WITH ME.

THESE INTERNATIONAL TAX LAWS HAVE REMAINED MUCH THE SAME FOR A HUNDRED YEARS.

BOTH THE GROUP OF EIGHT LEADING ECONOMIES IN THE WORLD (THE G8) AND THE EUROPEAN UNION HAVE PROPOSED TAX REFORMS...

BUT SO FAR IT'S NOT GONE MUCH BEYOND TALK.

I WONDER WHY.

THE LACK OF PROGRESS ON TAX REFORM MIRRORS THE STALLING OF DESPERATELY NEEDED CHANGES IN THE GLOBAL BANKING SECTOR.

AMONG THE COMPANIES THAT PAID NO CORPORATION TAX IN 2012 WAS ATOS.

WHAT DRIVES RIGHT-WING POLITICIANS TO IMPOVERISH THE POOR AND VULNERABLE WHILE BENEFITING THE ALREADY WEALTHY? IT IS THE CONSERVATIVE MORAL BELIEF THAT FAIRNESS MEANS PROPORTIONALITY.

YIPPEE!

FOR THOSE ON THE THE RIGHT, ECONOMIC EQUALITY MEANS OTHERS GETTING A SHARE OF THEIR MONEY. AS IT IS GOVERNMENT THAT REDISTRIBUTES THIS MONEY, THAT MAKES THE GOVERNMENT THE ENEMY.

THE POLITICAL RIGHT ARE INSTINCTIVELY ANTI-GOVERNMENT BECAUSE OF THIS, EVEN IF THEY ARE IN GOVERNMENT. IT ALSO EXPLAINS THEIR UNWILLINGNESS TO TACKLE THE PROBLEM OF TAX AVOIDANCE AND TAX FRAUD.

TAXATION IS IMMORAL.

THE STRONG MORALITY THEY HAVE BASED AROUND PROPORTIONALITY LEADS THEM TO FAVOUR FREE MARKETS AS AN ALTERNATIVE TO GOVERNMENTAL CONTROL.

THE ONLY WAY A GOVERNMENT CAN BE OF SERVICE TO NATIONAL PROSPERITY IS BY KEEPING ITS HANDS OFF.

POWER HAS BEEN HANDED OVER TO THOSE WHOSE MORAL VALUES ARE BASED ON RULES, OBEDIENCE, TRIBALISM, AND FEELINGS OF DISGUST.

A MORALITY BASED ON EMPATHY FOR THOSE LESS FORTUNATE THAN THEMSELVES IS CONSIDERED TO BE A SIGN OF PERSONAL WEAKNESS.

PARASITE!

HUNGRY

HERE'S AYN RAND ON SOCIAL WORKERS.

A PERSON WHO CHOOSES SOCIAL WORK AS A FULL-TIME PROFESSION CHOOSES TO DEVOTE HER LIFE TO THAT WHICH I DEFINE AS ZERO-WORSHIP...

TO HUMAN FLAWS, LACKS, FAILURES, MISERIES, VICES, AND EVILS. TO THE MORALLY, SPIRITUALLY, INTELLECTUALLY, PSYCHOLOGICALLY INFERIOR.

IF A PERSON WERE ACTUALLY MOTIVATED BY A LOVE OF VALUES AND A DESIRE TO RELIEVE HUMAN SUFFERING, SHE WOULD NOT BEGIN IN THE SLUMS AND WITH THE SUBNORMAL.

SHE WOULD LOOK AT WHAT OUR PRESENT SOCIETY DOES TO THE TALENTED, THE UNUSUAL, THE MENTALLY SUPERIOR CHILDREN...

IN SCHOOLS, IN COLLEGES, AND IN THEIR SUBSEQUENT CAREERS. SHE WOULD GO OUT TO FIGHT FOR THEM AND TO HELP THEM...

BEFORE THEY PERISH PSYCHOLOGICALLY IN LONELINESS AND BEWILDERMENT.

RAND WOULD, OF COURSE, CERTAINLY HAVE PLACED HERSELF IN THE TALENTED, UNUSUAL, AND MENTALLY SUPERIOR GROUPING.

SHE SPENT THE MAJORITY OF HER ADULT LIFE SEARCHING FOR A RATIONALE THROUGH WHICH SHE COULD PROMOTE SELFISHNESS AS A VIRTUE.

SELFISHNESS WAS PART OF HER CHARACTER, BUT SHE NEEDED AN INTELLECTUAL AND ECONOMIC ARGUMENT TO JUSTIFY IT.

MANY OF THOSE COMMITTED TO NEOLIBERALIST CAPITALISM TODAY DON'T APPEAR TO EVEN NEED RAND'S THIN ETHICAL FRAMEWORK TO EXCUSE THEIR BEHAVIOUR.

IT IS SEEN AS PERFECTLY ACCEPTABLE TO EXPLOIT PEOPLE AND RESOURCES...

WORK

WHIR!

CORRUPT GOVERNMENTS AND INSTITUTIONS...

AND DESPOIL THE ENVIRONMENT AT WILL.

THE VENERATION OF INDIVIDUALISM OVER COLLECTIVE RESPONSIBILITY HAS GIVEN THEM THE RIGHT TO DO WHATEVER THEY WISH...

YIPPEE!

WITH LITTLE STATE INTERFERENCE.

I DON'T CARE.

FOR EXAMPLE, A PHRASE IN THE US 1999 GRAMM-LEACH-BLILEY ACT (ALSO KNOWN AS THE FINANCIAL SERVICES MODERNIZATION ACT) MADE IT POSSIBLE FOR THE BANKING INDUSTRY TO REACH DEEP INTO THE REAL ECONOMY.

THIS PROVISION ALLOWED COMMERCIAL BANKS TO STEP OUTSIDE THE FINANCIAL WORLD AND BUY ASSETS THAT WOULD COMPLEMENT THEIR REGULAR BUSINESSES, SUCH AS PURCHASING A TRAVEL MAGAZINE IN ORDER TO PROMOTE CREDIT CARD USE. SOUNDS HARMLESS, DOESN'T IT?

IT ISN'T. BANKERS AND THEIR LAWYERS HAVE INTERPRETED THIS PROVISION IN A WAY THAT HAS GONE FAR BEYOND MERE PROMOTION. TODAY, BANKS LIKE MORGAN STANLEY, J.P. MORGAN CHASE, AND GOLDMAN SACHS OWN OIL TANKERS, RUN AIRPORTS, AND CONTROL HUGE QUANTITIES OF COAL, NATURAL GAS, HEATING OIL, ELECTRIC POWER, AND PRECIOUS METALS.

THEY ARE BUYING WHOLE INDUSTRIAL PROCESSES. THIS INCLUDES OIL STILL IN THE GROUND, THE TANKERS NEEDED TO MOVE IT ACROSS THE SEA, THE REFINERIES THAT TURN IT INTO FUEL, AND THE PIPELINES THAT BRING IT TO OUR CITIES AND CARS. THIS IS THE INFRASTRUCTURE OF THE MODERN WORLD.

THE EVENTS OF 2008 HAVE NOT TEMPERED THE FINANCIAL INDUSTRY'S APPETITE FOR CRIMINAL ACTIVITY. SINCE THEN, BARCLAYS, CITIGROUP, J.P. MORGAN CHASE, UBS, AND GOLDMAN SACHS HAVE ALL BEEN IMPLICATED IN THE MANIPULATION OF THE LONDON INTERBANK OFFERED RATE (LIBOR). THIS CREATED HIGHER COSTS FOR PENSION FUNDS, MUTUAL FUNDS, AND ANYONE WHO BOUGHT AND SOLD CURRENCY.

IN 2012, HSBC, EUROPE'S LARGEST BANK, WAS OBLIGED TO PAY $1.4 BILLION IN PENALTIES TO SETTLE A US MONEY LAUNDERING PROBE. THIS INVESTIGATION FOCUSED ON THE MOVEMENT OF MILLIONS OF DOLLARS ON BEHALF OF MEXICAN DRUG CARTELS. IT'S WORTH POINTING OUT THAT HSBC STILL MADE A PRE-TAX PROFIT OF $20.6 BILLION THAT YEAR.

WHY IS THIS NOT CONSIDERED TO BE ORGANISED CRIME? HAVING BEATEN COMMUNISM, CAPITALISM IS WELL ON ITS WAY TO DEFEATING DEMOCRACY ITSELF. THE POST-FINANCIAL-CRISIS WORLD SHOULD HAVE SEEN A RUSH TO REIN IN THE POWER OF THE BANKS, BUT THIS HAS NOT HAPPENED.

INSTEAD, GOVERNMENTS HAVE ESSENTIALLY BEEN CAPTURED BY BIG BUSINESS TO DO THEIR BIDDING. THIS IS DISASTROUS, BECAUSE ANY SOCIETY THAT ALLOWS PREDATORY, VALUE-DESTROYING BEHAVIOUR TO BECOME MORE PROFITABLE THAN HONEST WORK RISKS EVERYTHING.

IN THE US TODAY, MORE THAN 21 MILLION PEOPLE ARE IN NEED OF FULL-TIME WORK, MANY RUNNING OUT OF JOBLESS BENEFITS, WHILE THE FINANCIAL CLASS POCKETS RECORD PROFITS, AND SPENDS LAVISHLY ON CAMPAIGNS TO SECURE A POLITICAL ORDER THAT SERVES ITS INTERESTS, WHILE DEMANDING FURTHER AUSTERITY MEASURES.

WHERE AMERICA GOES, OTHER WESTERN COUNTRIES TEND TO FOLLOW. WHAT WE ARE SEEING HERE IS THE ECONOMIC SUBJECTION OF THE MAJORITY BY LARGE CORPORATIONS AND THE SUPER-RICH. THE DEMOCRATIC STATE, WHICH IS THE ONLY THING THAT CAN KEEP THE UNCARING BILLIONAIRE CLASS IN CHECK, HAS BEEN CORRUPTED OR IS SHRINKING AWAY.

TEA PARTIERS MAY SHARE THE KOCH BROTHERS' DISLIKE OF TAXES AND BIG GOVERNMENT. BUT THERE IS A DIFFERENCE BETWEEN MAINSTREAM CONSERVATISM AND A FRINGE AGENDA THAT FAVOURS BIG BUSINESS AND THE SUPER-RICH.

THE TENS OF THOUSANDS WHO TURNED OUT TO CALL FOR A REDUCTION IN GOVERNMENT SPENDING AND TAXATION DO NOT WANT TO FALL INTO POVERTY, HAVE THEIR CHILDREN RECEIVE A POOR-QUALITY EDUCATION, OR GET INADEQUATE HEALTH CARE, BUT THIS IS WHAT A SMALLER STATE WOULD MEAN. TEA PARTIERS ARE UNWITTINGLY PUSHING THE SELFISH INTERESTS OF GIANT CORPORATIONS, NOT PEOPLE.

AYN RAND DREAMED OF A WORLD UNHINDERED BY REGULATION, GOVERNMENT, OR CONCERN FOR THE DISADVANTAGED.

MANY OF THE PEOPLE WHO FOLLOW HER PHILOSOPHY DON'T APPEAR TO REALISE, OR PERHAPS CARE, THAT THESE IDEAS WOULD CREATE A GROTESQUELY UNFAIR SOCIETY.

AMERICA TODAY HAS A SHRINKING MIDDLE CLASS, AN INCREASINGLY DOMINANT BILLIONAIRE ELITE, AND A GOVERNMENT CORRUPTED BY VAST AMOUNTS OF MONEY.

ALL THE INGREDIENTS ARE IN PLACE TO CREATE A NEW GILDED AGE IN WHICH THE COMMANDING HEIGHTS OF THE ECONOMY ARE CONTROLLED, NOT BY TALENTED INDIVIDUALS, BUT BY FAMILY DYNASTIES.

THIS CORRUPTED ENVIRONMENT HAS GENERATED A FEELING OF POLITICAL DISCONNECTION AMONG ORDINARY PEOPLE. A DESPAIR THAT ONLY BENEFITS THOSE WHO WANT TO KEEP THE ECONOMY RIGGED TOWARDS THOSE WHO ARE ALREADY WEALTHY.

WHAT'S THE POINT IN VOTING?

THE CORPORATE ELITE COUNT ON THE PUBLIC'S APATHY TO PROTECT THEIR PERSONAL ASSETS AND BUSINESSES FROM FAIR COMPETITION, EFFECTIVE REGULATION, AND TAXATION.

ALL POLITICAL PARTIES ARE MUCH THE SAME.

IN RECENT TIMES, WHEN THE PUBLIC'S ANGER HAS TURNED TO POLITICAL ACTION, AS WITH THE TEA PARTY OR UKIP, IT HAS BEEN EITHER AIMED AT THE WRONG TARGET, OR, LIKE THE OCCUPY MOVEMENT, HAS FAILED TO CATCH THE IMAGINATION OF THE WIDER POPULATION.

BLOODY HIPPIES!

DAILY MAIL

IF THE PUBLIC'S OUTRAGE COULD BE DIRECTED AT THOSE ACTUALLY RESPONSIBLE FOR LOW WAGES, RISING HOUSING COSTS, AND A CORRUPTED POLITICAL SYSTEM, INSTEAD OF THOSE ALSO BEING VICTIMISED, SUCH AS MIGRANT WORKERS AND THE UNEMPLOYED, THEN PERHAPS REAL CHANGE COULD BE ACHIEVED?

LIKE THAT'S GOING TO HAPPEN.

IT'S A MISTAKE TO THINK THAT THE CURRENT POLITICAL CIRCUMSTANCES ARE SET IN STONE.

MANY TIMES IN THE PAST, CITIZENS' MOVEMENTS, COMPOSED OF PEOPLE FROM ALL LEVELS OF SOCIETY, HAVE BROUGHT ABOUT MAJOR CHANGE.

WITHOUT THESE CAMPAIGNS THERE WOULD BE NO CHILD LABOUR LAWS, NO UNIVERSAL PUBLIC EDUCATION, NO ENVIRONMENTAL PROTECTION LAWS, AND NO WOMAN'S SUFFRAGE. IN THE US SOUTHERN STATES, RACIAL SEGREGATION WOULD NEVER HAVE BEEN ABOLISHED. SLAVERY WOULD HAVE CONTINUED.

THESE SOCIAL MOVEMENTS FACED SEEMINGLY IMPOSSIBLE ODDS. THEY EXISTED IN A TIME WHEN IT MUST HAVE LOOKED AS IF NOTHING COULD POSSIBLY CHANGE, SUCH WERE THE VESTED INTERESTS RANGED AGAINST THEM. YET THEY SUCCEEDED ANYWAY.

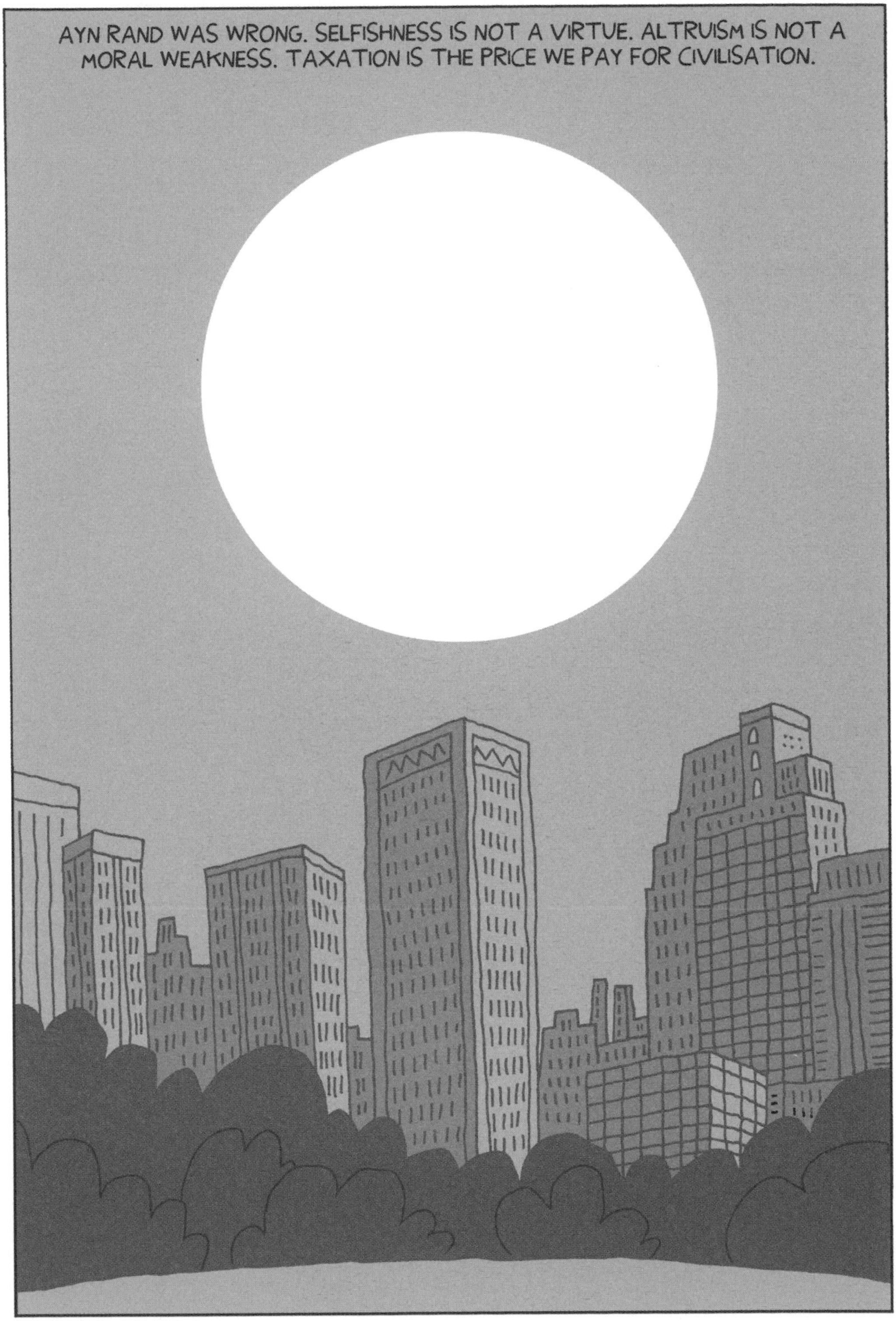
AYN RAND WAS WRONG. SELFISHNESS IS NOT A VIRTUE. ALTRUISM IS NOT A MORAL WEAKNESS. TAXATION IS THE PRICE WE PAY FOR CIVILISATION.

IT'S TIME WE REJECTED THIS SELFISH PHILOSOPHY.

S O U R C E S :

AYN RAND

Weiss G. *Ayn Rand Nation: The Hidden Struggle for America's Soul.* New York: St Martin's Griffin; 2013.

Heller AC. *Ayn Rand and the World She Made.* New York: Anchor Books; 2009.

Burns J. *Goddess of the Market: Ayn Rand and the American Right.* New York: Oxford University Press; 2009.

Mallon T. Possessed: Did Ayn Rand's cult outstrip her canon? *New Yorker.* 2009 Nov 9. www.newyorker.com/reporting/2009/11/09/091109fa_fact_mallon (accessed 2013 Sept 13).

Greenspan A. *The Age of Turbulence: Adventures in a New World.* New York: Penguin; 2007.

Branden B. *The Passion of Ayn Rand.* New York: Doubleday; 1998.

Rand A. *Atlas Shrugged.* London: Penguin Classics; 2007.

Rand A. *The Fountainhead.* London: Penguin Classics; 2007.

Rand A. *We The Living.* London: Penguin Classics; 2007.

THE CRASH

Lewis M. *The Big Short: Inside the Doomsday Machine.* London: Penguin; 2011.

Lancaster J. *Whoops! Why Everyone Owes Everyone and No One Can Pay.* London: Penguin; 2010.

Stiglitz J. *Freefall: Free Markets and the Sinking of the Global Economy.* London: Penguin; 2010.

Tett G. *Fool's Gold: How Unrestrained Greed Corrupted a Dream, Shattered Global Markets and Unleashed a Catastrophe.* London: Abacus; 2010.

McLean B, Nocera J. *All the Devils Are Here: Unmasking the Men Who Bankrupted the World.* London: Portfolio Penguin; 2010.

Madrick J. How Alan Greenspan Helped Wreck the Economy. *Rolling Stone.* 2011 June 16. www.rollingstone.com/politics/blogs/national-affairs/how-alan-greenspan-helped-wreck-the-economy-20110616/ (accessed 2013 June 12).

Prosecuting Wall Street. *60 Minutes.* 2011 Dec 05. www.cbsnews.com/news/prosecuting-wall-street (accessed 2013 Sept 20).

Interview with Brooksley Born. *Frontline.* 2009 Oct 20. www.pbs.org/wgbh/pages/frontline/warning/interviews/born.html (accessed 2013 Sept 23).

Taibbi M. The People vs. Goldman Sachs. *Rolling Stone.* 2011 May 11. www.rollingstone.com/politics/news/the-people-vs-goldman-sachs-20110511 (accessed 2013 Sept 23).

Cohan WD. How Goldman Killed A.I.G. *New York Times.* 2011 Feb 16. http://opinionator.blogs.nytimes.com/2011/02/16/ how-goldman-killed-a-i-g-and-other-stories/?_php=true&_type=blogs&_r=1 (accessed 2013 Sept 23).

Balzli B. Greek Debt Crisis: How Goldman Sachs Helped Greece to Mask its True Debt. *Spiegel Online International.* 2010 Feb 8. www.spiegel.de/international/europe/greek-debt-crisis-how-goldman-sachs-helped-greece-to-mask-its-true-debt-a-676634.html (accessed 2013 Sept 25).

Cahoon S. Wall Street Revolving Door. *Too Big Has Failed.* 2013 May 30. www.toobighasfailed.org/wall-street-revolving-door (accessed 2013 Sept 25).

Thompson D. Christopher Warren, Fraud Suspect, Caught At Border With $70,000 In Cowboy Boots, $1M In Swiss Bank Certificates. *Huffington Post.* 2009 Nov 2. www.huffingtonpost.com/2009/02/12/christopher-warren-fraud-_n_166340.html (accessed 2013 Sept 16).

Smith G. Why I Am Leaving Goldman Sachs. *New York Times.* 2012 March 14. www.nytimes.com/2012/03/14/opinion/why-i-am-leaving-goldman-sachs.html?pagewanted= all (accessed 2013 Sept 18).

Ensor J. How the City bankrolls the Conservatives. *Telegraph.* 2010 Oct 1. www.telegraph.co.uk/news/politics/8800457/How-the-City-bankrolls-the-Conservatives.html (accessed 2013 Dec 18).

THE AGE OF SELFISHNESS

Mooney C. *The Republican Brain: The Science of Why They Deny Science – And Reality.* New Jersey: John Wiley & Sons; 2012.

Pinker S. *The Better Angels of Our Nature: A History of Violence and Humanity.* London: Allen Lane; 2011.

Paramaguru K. Britain's Breadline: Austerity Leads to Growing Ranks of the Hungry. *Time.* 2013 Nov 22. http://world.time.com/2013/11/22/britains-breadline-austerity-leads-to-growing-ranks-of-the-hungry (accessed 2013 Nov 22).

Walker P. Benefit cuts are fuelling abuse of disabled people, say charities. *Guardian.* 2012 Feb 5. www.theguardian.com/society/2012/feb/05/benefit-cuts-fuelling-abuse-disabled-people (accessed 2013 Nov 24).

Taylor K. UKIP's Stance on the City Undermines Its Anti-Establishment Rhetoric. *Huffington Post.* 2014 April 30. www.huffingtonpost.co.uk/keith-taylor/ukips-stance-on-the-city-_b_5239470.html (accessed 2014 May 1).

Jones A. Tea Party: Palin's Pet, Or Is There More To It Underneath? *Money Talk.* 2010 Oct 5. www.usmoneytalk.com/finance/tea-party-palins-pet-or-is-there-more-to-it-underneath-910/ (accessed 2014 May 1).

Rich F. The Billionaires Bankrolling the Tea Party. *New York Times.* 2010 Aug 28. www.nytimes.com/2010/08/29/opinion/29rich.html?_r=0 (accessed 2014 May 1).

Rick Santelli: Tea Party. *Freedom Eden.* 2009 Feb 19. http://freedomeden.blogspot.co.uk/2009/02/rick-santelli-tea-party.html (accessed 2014 May 1).

Paul Sykes: the man spending millions to make Ukip's posters visible from space. *Guardian.* 2014 April 23. www.theguardian.com/politics/shortcuts/2014/apr/23/paul-sykes-ukip-britain-out-of-europe (accessed 2014 May 1).

UKIP Threat To Workers' Rights Exposed. *GMB.* 2014 May 2. www.gmb.org.uk/newsroom/ukip-threat-to-workers-rights-exposed (accessed 2014 May 5).

Bloodworth J. Coalition presides over shocking increase in number of people using food banks. *Left Foot Forward.* 2013 April 23. www.leftfootforward.org/2013/04/coalition-presides-over-1000-increase-in-number-of-people-using-food-banks (accessed 2013 June 14).

Rogers S. UK welfare spending: how much does each benefit really cost? *Guardian.* 2013 Jan 8. www.theguardian.com/news/datablog/2013/jan/08/uk-benefit-welfare-spending (accessed 2013 June 14).

Glaze B. Linda Wootton: Double heart and lung transplant dies nine days after she has benefits stopped. *Mirror.* 2013 May 26. http://www.mirror.co.uk/news/uk-news/linda-wootton-double-heart-lung-1912498 (accessed 2013 Sept 14).

Atos Disability Benefits Row: Epileptic Colin Traynor's Death Blamed On Stress Of Being Found Fit For Work. *Huffington Post.* 2012 Sept 26. http://www.huffingtonpost.co.uk/2012/09/26/atos-disability-benefits-colin-traynor-epilepsy-_n_1917042.html (accessed 2013 Sept 14).

Ramesh R. Atos apologises to long-term sick wrongly assessed as fit for work. *Guardian.* 2013 April 17. www.theguardian.com/society/2013/apr/17/atos-apologises-long-term-sick (accessed 2013 Sept 14).

Ryan F. Rod Liddle's attack on disability cannot be ignored. *Guardian.* 2012 Jan 30. www.theguardian.com/commentisfree/2012/jan/30/rod-liddle-attack-disability (accessed 2013 Sept 14).

McDonald C. Heartbroken dad blames benefits axemen for driving his ill son to commit suicide. *Daily Record.* 2013 Sept 13. www.dailyrecord.co.uk/news/scottish-news/heartbroken-dad-blames-benefits-axemen-2292176 (accessed 2013 Sept 14).

Taibbi M. The Vampire Squid Strikes Again: The Mega Banks' Most Devious Scam Yet. *Rolling Stone.* 2014 Feb 12. www.rollingstone.com/politics/news/the-vampire-squid-strikes-again-the-mega-banks-most-devious-scam-yet-20140212 (accessed 2014 Feb 12).

asset
Something owned by an individual or business that has economic value in terms of income or capital gain. The main asset classes are cash, stocks/shares, bonds and property.

bailout
The emergency rescue of a company or bank in difficulty.

base rate
The lowest rate at which a bank will charge interest, set by a country's central bank and used to control inflation.

bond
A loan or IOU, also called a 'fixed-interest security' or 'debt instrument'. Companies, banks, and governments use bonds to borrow money from investors, usually to finance expenditure or expansion. The issuer pays the bondholder interest at regular dates, and then repays the whole sum on a fixed future date. Banks and investors buy and trade bonds.

capital
For individuals, 'capital' refers to their financial assets or the financial value of those assets. For companies, it refers to sources of financing such as new shares or bonds, or to factories, machinery and equipment. For banks, it refers to their ability to absorb losses (known as 'capital adequacy'). If a bank runs out of capital, then it will become insolvent.

central bank
A country's central bank has responsibility for setting the base interest rate, controlling the money supply, and acting as banker to other banks. The US central bank is the Federal Reserve. In the UK, it is the Bank of England.

collateralised debt obligation (CDO)
A structured financial product that pools individual income-producing loans, bonds or other assets into a bundle, which can then be sold to investors. The pooled assets, such as mortgages and loans, are debt obligations that are backed by collateral. The CDO has various 'tranches' with different levels of risk, and can be assigned a higher credit rating than the individual assets, as the risk is diversified and spread.

commodity
Commodities are raw products that have a common market price and can be traded on a stock exchange in fixed quantities. The commodities markets range from wheat, cotton, sugar, and cocoa to industrial metals such as iron ore and copper, and energy products such as oil and natural gas.

credit default swap (CDS)
A financial contract that arranges the transfer of risk from one party to another. A lender faces the risk of default by a second party, the borrower, before the loan is repaid, and a third party agrees to insure this risk in return for periodic payments.

credit rating
An assessment, made by a specialist credit rating agency, of the creditworthiness of a borrower, such as a company or a government, based on its ability to repay. Ratings range from a top AAA rating down to D. Ratings of BBB-minus or above are considered 'investment grade'.

default
A default occurs when a borrower fails to meet the terms of a loan or other debt, either by missing an interest payment or by failing to repay the capital.

derivative
A security whose price is based on the price of an underlying investment such as a commodity, currency or share index. It provides a way of investing in a particular product without having to own it directly, and of benefiting from losses as well as gains in asset prices. Derivatives allow investors to hedge their risks, but also to speculate on markets.

float
Flotation on a stock market is the process of changing a private company into a public one by issuing and selling shares. Flotation is another way (as well as bonds) for companies to obtain financing from outside the company to fund a project or expansion. Widely called 'going public' in the US.

foreclosure
Where a homeowner is unable to make full payments on their mortgage, this allows the lender to take back the property and sell the home. Called 'repossession' in the UK.

future
A mechanism by which a standard quantity of a commodity can be bought or sold in the future at a price agreed today, without the full value of the transaction being settled at the outset. It could be used to hedge or to speculate on the price. Futures contracts are traded on a stock exchange.

gross domestic product (GDP)
The most commonly used measure of a country's output or economic activity, including goods and services. Generally

calculated as a total of consumer spending, government spending, investment and exports, minus imports.

hedge

To 'hedge' is to make an investment specifically in order to mitigate the risk of adverse price movements in the value of an asset. Futures contracts, which fix prices in advance, or more complex derivatives such as options, are typically used for hedging.

hedge fund

A private investment fund with very high minimum investment levels and high fees, which was originally devised in order principally to eliminate or reduce risk. However, innovation in the derivatives markets has resulted in a wide range of hedge funds using complex strategies that place greater emphasis on producing above-average, highly leveraged returns rather than on controlling risk.

leverage

Leveraging, or (in the UK) 'gearing', means borrowing money to add to your own in order to make a larger investment. This approach can greatly improve returns when markets are rising, but, equally, will greatly increase losses when markets fall. Therefore leveraging increases risk as well as reward.

liquidity

The ease with which something can be converted into cash. A bank account, for example, is more liquid than property, which will take time to sell.

liquidity crisis

Essentially, for companies, a cash flow problem that may lead to bankruptcy. In wider, more national terms, this refers to a situation in which it suddenly becomes much more difficult for banks to obtain cash. For example, worrying financial news may cause investors and depositors to withdraw their cash from banks all at once, or banks may stop making loans to businesses, or may even cease lending to each other. If a bank runs out of cash it will collapse, which has a negative ripple effect throughout the economy, therefore countries' central banks usually respond to a liquidity crisis by providing emergency bailout cash loans to the struggling bank.

mutual fund

An investment vehicle made up of a pool of money collected from multiple small investors in order to invest more significant amounts of capital in securities such as shares, bonds, and other assets. A fund gives small investors access to professionally managed, diversified portfolios of securities that would be hard to create with a small amount of money. In the UK, mutual funds are commonly known as 'collective investment schemes', or by their separate types, such as 'investment trusts' or 'open-ended investment companies'.

negative equity

A situation in which the value of a property falls below the amount of the mortgage that still has to be paid off.

security

Any financial instrument, such as an asset or a derivatives contract, that can be assigned a value and then traded. It could be a stock or share, a bond, or a CDO. The term is usually seen in the plural, i.e. 'securities'.

Entirely separately, the term 'security' is also used to mean something that is offered as collateral by a borrower when taking out a 'secured' loan, such as a mortgage.

securitisation

The process of creating a single, tradeable security by combining various individual assets or loans. For example, the debts from a number of mortgages can be combined to make a mortgage-backed security, which is a type of CDO. Investors who own these receive a regular stream of income from the monthly mortgage payments.

stock

A type of security that represents a proportional unit of ownership in a company and carries a claim on part of its assets and earnings. More commonly known in the UK as 'shares' or 'equity'. Being a shareholder entitles the holder to a share in any profits, in the form of dividends declared, and may carry voting rights.

While shares are often used to refer to the stock of a corporation, they can also signify ownership of mutual funds.

toxic debts/loans

Debts or loans where default is expected, i.e. where money lent out becomes unlikely to be paid back. Most lenders expect that a certain small percentage of their borrowers will not be able to repay; 'toxic debt' is reserved for a situation where an entire bundle of loans is unlikely to be repaid.

SOURCES

Investopedia. www.investopedia.com/dictionary.
Finance Glossary, www.finance-glossary.com

MORE FROM MYRIAD

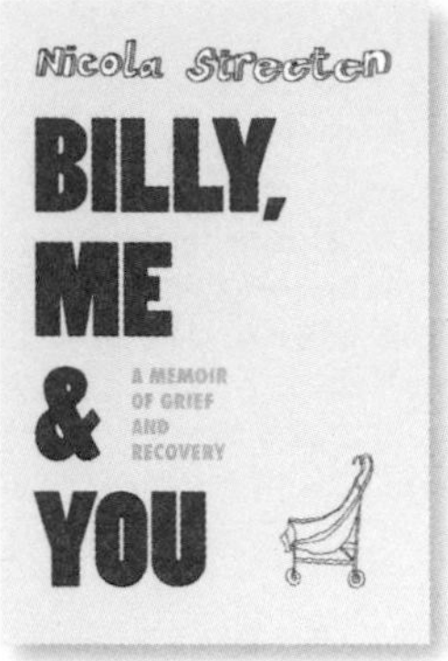
Nicola Streeten
BILLY, ME & YOU
A MEMOIR OF GRIEF AND RECOVERY

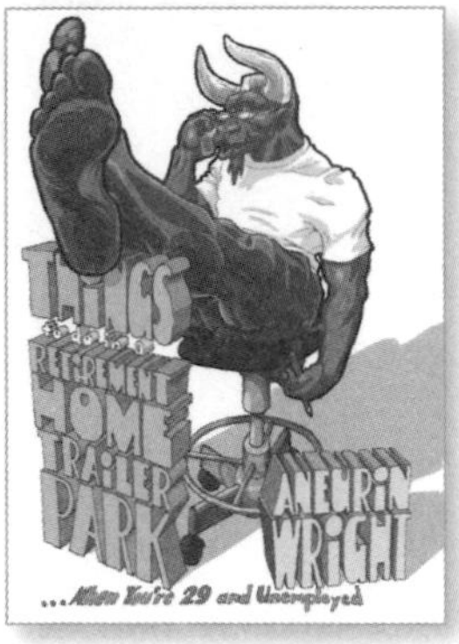
THINGS TO DO IN A RETIREMENT HOME TRAILER PARK
ANEURIN WRIGHT
...When You're 29 and Unemployed

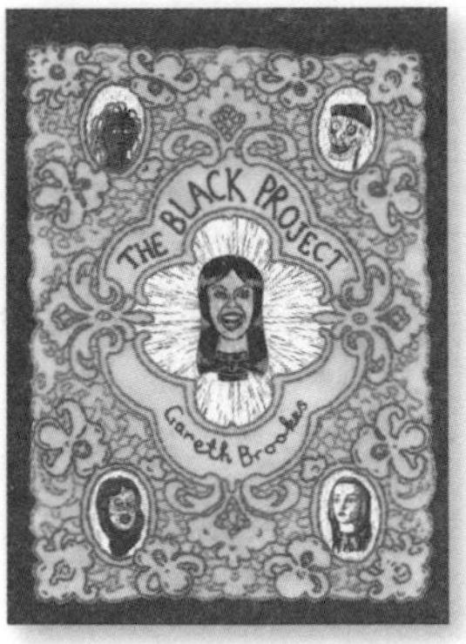
THE BLACK PROJECT
Gareth Brookes

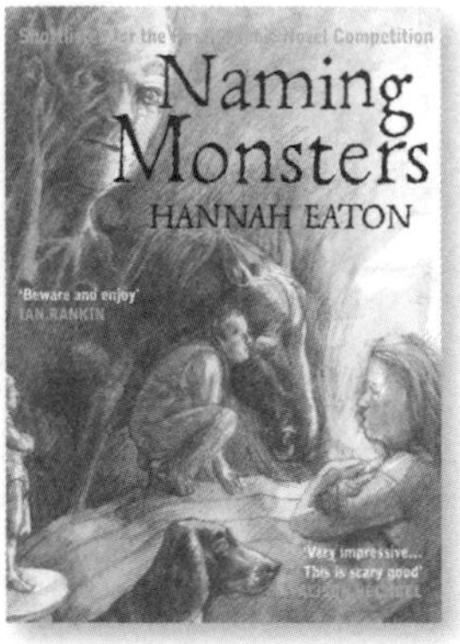
Naming Monsters
HANNAH EATON
'Beware and enjoy'
IAN RANKIN
'Very impressive... This is scary good'

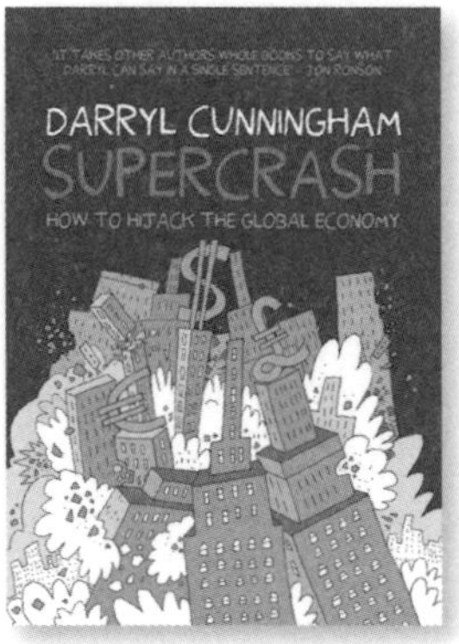
DARRYL CUNNINGHAM
SUPERCRASH
HOW TO HIJACK THE GLOBAL ECONOMY

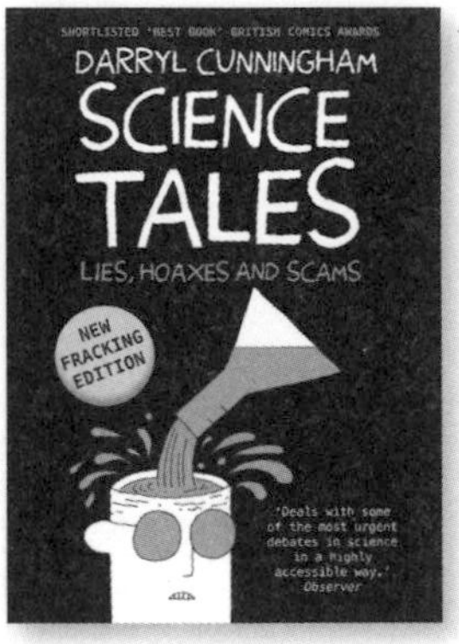
SHORTLISTED 'BEST BOOK' BRITISH COMICS AWARDS
DARRYL CUNNINGHAM
SCIENCE TALES
LIES, HOAXES AND SCAMS
NEW FRACKING EDITION
'Deals with some of the most urgent debates in science in a highly accessible way.' Observer

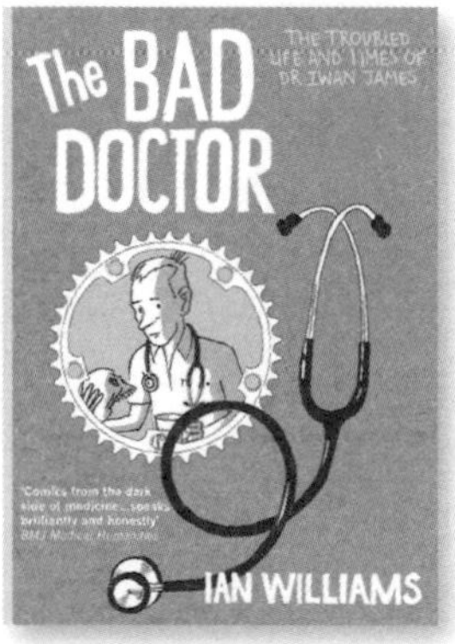
The BAD DOCTOR
THE TROUBLED LIFE AND TIMES OF DR IWAN JAMES
IAN WILLIAMS

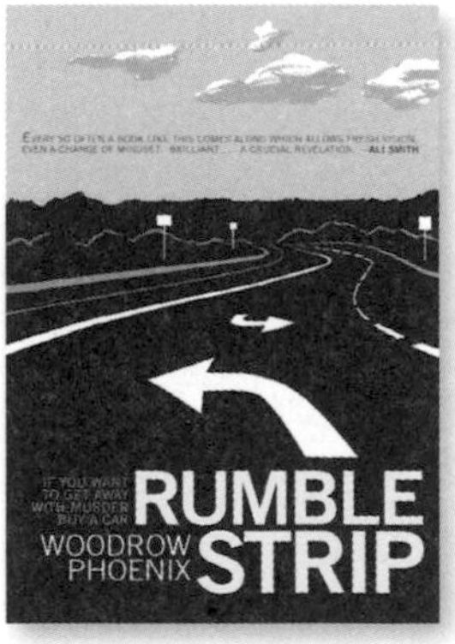
RUMBLE STRIP
WOODROW PHOENIX

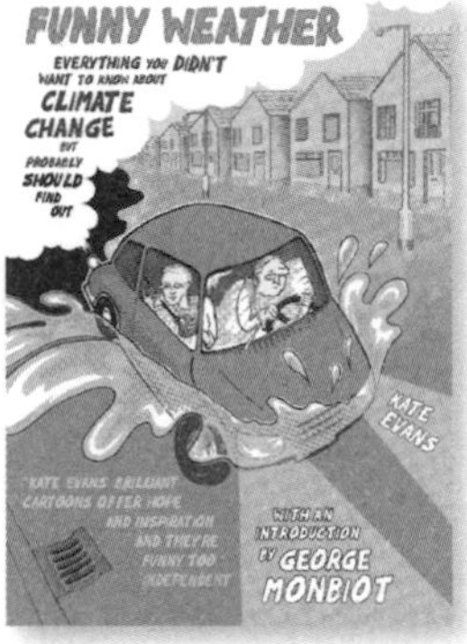
FUNNY WEATHER
EVERYTHING YOU DIDN'T WANT TO KNOW ABOUT CLIMATE CHANGE BUT PROBABLY SHOULD FIND OUT
KATE EVANS
WITH AN INTRODUCTION BY GEORGE MONBIOT

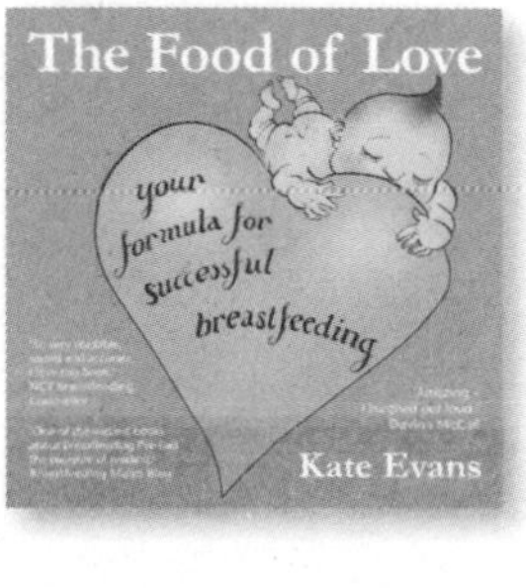
The Food of Love
your formula for successful breastfeeding
Kate Evans

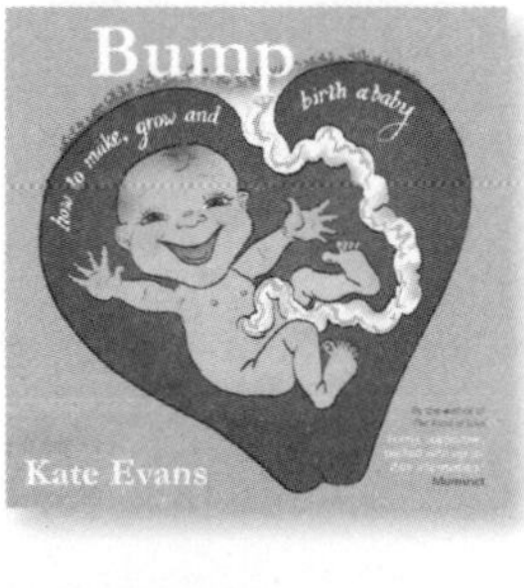
Bump
how to make, grow and birth a baby
Kate Evans

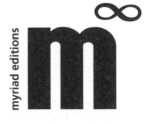

myriad editions